THE GUILT-FREE GUIDE TO

greening YOUR HOLIDAYS

HOW TO DUMP THE ECO GUILT
AND MAKE GOING GREEN FUN AND EASY
FOR THE WHOLE FAMILY

DONNA DEFORBES

Eco-Mothering
DonnaDeForbesCreates.com

ISBN-13 978-1512041156
ISBN-10 1512041157

Book design, cover design and infographics by
www.DonnaDeForbesCreates.com

Author photos by Scott Indermaur
Cover and chapter photos from DepositPhotos.com

Printed by CreateSpace, Charleston, SC.
Available on Amazon.com, Kindle and other retail outlets.

This book is dedicated to my daughter, Sofie, who rocked my world seven years ago. She was the inspiration behind my Eco-Mothering blog and continues to challenge and amaze me every day.

Table *of* Contents

Introduction

What Does "Guilt-Free" Mean?

Are you perfectly green? Me neither. But we don't have to feel guilty about it. In fact, we shouldn't feel guilty about it, because guilt is a surefire way to ruin any commitment to ecological change. Huh?

Yes, cultivating an environmentally conscious attitude is important. But what's even more important is to feel good about doing it. If you're motivated by guilt or fear from external sources, like doomsday news reports, your actions won't last long. It's interior motivation *(this is aligned with my values and feels good!)* that makes for lasting change.

Although going green can seem overwhelming and full of "shoulds," there are ways to make it fun and easy for the whole family. "Guilt-free" means accepting your imperfection while still making conscious choices every day.

We need to be informed about our options and our impact before we can choose what feels good to us. And while we may not choose the greenest option in every scenario, that's okay. The joy you emit in the actions that you *do* take will have a bigger impact because of it.

The Heart of the Holidays

I focused this book on holidays because they are so often filled with excess. Yet holidays are also steeped in strong traditions (familial and cultural) that often prevent us from feeling we can make changes.

For this reason, I begin each chapter by delving into the history of the holiday. Why do we make New Year's resolutions? Who was St. Valentine? What is the origin of trick-or-treating? You might be surprised to discover that some traditions we follow are from ancient cultures and practices you didn't expect.

Our American Christmas, for example, was "reinvented" in the 19th century by pulling customs from a variety of countries and eras. Knowing this makes it easier to choose which holiday traditions you want to keep and which you can discard.

Traditions give us context and guidelines. They connect us to the generations before us, both genealogically and culturally. But that doesn't mean we must follow them verbatim, particularly if they don't ring true for us. That makes them hollow.

As you'll see, our holidays have evolved over centuries; tweaking traditions to add our own personal flavor makes us part of their ongoing evolution.

Holidays carry lots of weight in our culture. We like to celebrate big and spend money on gifts, food and decoration. There's nothing wrong with that. These holidays have their roots in ancient cultures that also celebrated big with gifts, food and decoration. However, because of their lack of modern conveniences, those cultures usually had a stronger connection to the earth. They maintained a balance between their needs and the planet's. That's the piece that has gotten lost along the way: balance.

This book digs beneath surface traditions to the heart of a holiday. Is it really about presents... candy... turkey? Or is it about joy... rebirth... gratitude? Many of us fall into the trap of doing what we grew up doing or what everyone else is doing without considering whether it really works for our family. Maintaining someone else's standards can be stressful.

The Guilt-Free Guide to Greening Your Holidays is just that: a guide. It offers ideas for eco-friendly celebration from January through December.

Take only what appeals to you. Do as little or as much as you want. Perhaps you'll discover ways to reduce your disposable waste. Or maybe you'll incorporate some earth-based elements into what's typically a commercial holiday for you. Sometimes all it takes is understanding the essence of a holiday to become clear on how you'd really like to celebrate it.

DID YOU KNOW?

Little actions *do* make a difference. Here's an example: one person recycling a six-foot stack of newspapers saves the life of one 35-foot tree. Pretty amazing, huh?

What's *in this* Book

- History and meaning of a holiday
- Tips for greening holiday traditions
- Out-of-the-box celebration ideas
- Interesting holiday stats and Top 5 lists
- Green resources

Each chapter lists ways to green typical American holiday traditions and introduces alternative avenues of celebration. Many of these ideas will also save you money and keep your family healthier.

Don't fall into the trap of believing you need to be super-eco by following every suggestion. Remember, we're dumping the guilt. These are merely ideas for inspiration. Every action you take—no matter how small it may seem to you—affects positive results. Focus on what you're passionate about, because taking action joyfully is the key to lasting change.

My Story

I grew up with typical American holiday celebrations: twinkle lights and tinsel, plastic Easters, handmade cards and hand-traced turkeys, and piles of presents. Most traditions I enjoyed, most I never even thought about, and I expected to do the same for my kids.

Then in my early twenties, my fiancé and I moved away from my family, away from my home state and the suburban culture I grew up in. That geographic shift helped shift my world view. I met new people, new customs, new ways of thinking. I was introduced to Filipino customs from my in-laws. I made friends with self-proclaimed witches who celebrated Solstices. I met Indian, Chinese and Latino friends who exposed me to their cultural practices. While my husband and I maintained some of our families' holiday traditions out of nostalgia, we also created new ones.

The Solstices were my first step in celebrating non-traditional holidays. Their earth focus appealed to my love for nature, and I found a fresh joy in diverging from old routines. (Summer Solstice scarf dancing anyone?)

Author, Donna DeForbes, with her husband and daughter in 2013.

Becoming a mother caused me to really question the meaning behind traditional holiday practices. Did I want to bestow mounds of candy on my daughter at Easter and Halloween? Was Christmas going to be all about presents and being "good?" No thanks. But what traditions would replace them?

I wanted my daughter to grow into a concerned, active resident of the earth, and I knew our actions spoke volumes. Because holidays often act as the pinnacles of our daily lives, it seemed important that my family absorb them into our eco-conscious tendencies. So I decided to read up on how these holidays began, what they really meant and how other cultures celebrated them.

Over the years, my family has crafted a balance in our holiday celebrations. We host an annual Winter Solstice party with a drum circle and outdoor caroling; we also celebrate Christmas with Santa Claus and gifts. We've been introduced to Chinese New Year performances and local May Day festivals just as we share our American Thanksgiving traditions with our dear friends from India. We always recycle; we sometimes eat organic; we'll never go vegetarian.

We are far from perfect. We incorporate only those eco elements that bring us joy. Because of this, they are easily assimilated into our holidays, and they usually last for years.

My point is this: The holidays don't need to be stressful for us *or* the earth. We can find balance in our celebrations while still reaping joy. In general, when we do what feels good naturally, we stress less, spend less and use less of the earth's resources.

From Blog to Book

This book came out of my blog, Eco-Mothering, which I founded in 2008 and curated for eight years. With a focus on natural parenting and eco-friendly living, Eco-Mothering.com introduced thousands of readers on ways to make going green fun and easy for the whole family. It is my hope that this book will do the same.

Happy celebrating!

Donna

Chapter 1:
New Year's

History *and* Meaning

Cultures around the globe have been celebrating the start of a new year since at least 2,000 B.C. when the Babylonians marked the season with an eleven-day festival (for them, it was the first new moon after the spring equinox).

Ancient cultures typically started a calendar year with an earth-based agricultural or astronomical event. Egyptians saw their New Year begin with the annual summer flooding of the Nile River. The lunar-based Chinese New Year originated as a celebration of the spring planting season. The Persian New Year,

Nowruz, was a 13-day spring festival held around the vernal equinox, and it's still celebrated today in Iran, Asia and other areas of the Middle East.

How January 1 Became New Year's Day

The ancient Romans also followed the tradition of beginning the year in spring. Their ten-month calendar began March 1 until Julius Caesar introduced the Julian calendar, which was more in sync with the sun. January 1 was selected as the new starting date for two reasons: to honor Janus, the Roman god of beginnings, and because it was the start of the civil year when newly elected Roman consuls began their tenure. (Interestingly, the original ten-month calendar still shows in our month names: *octo* is Latin for "eight," *novem* for "nine" and *decem* for "ten.")

Outside of the Roman Empire, January 1 wasn't officially recognized as New Year's Day until 1582 with "Gregorian calendar reform." Taking leap years into consideration, the Church-approved Gregorian calendar was even more aligned with the sun. However, some countries—including Great Britain and the American colonies—still celebrated New Year's in March and did not adopt the Gregorian calendar until 1752.

New Year's Traditions Around the World, Then...

In ancient times, people celebrated the New Year with a variety of festivals. The Babylonians participated in parades and religious role-playing. The concept of making New Year's resolutions can be traced back to the Babylonians who promised to pay off debts and return borrowed farm equipment in order to please the gods at the start of a new year.

The Egyptians honored the time with religious rites... alongside raucous music, parties, feasts and beer. Early Christians used New Year's Day to reflect on past mistakes and find ways to improve oneself for the coming year. The Romans offered sacrifices to the god Janus, decorated homes with laurel branches, exchanged gifts of figs and honey and often worked part of the day because idleness was seen as a bad way to begin the year.

The traditional Chinese New Year was the most important holiday of their year. Businesses closed while people gathered with family to clean and clear their homes of bad energy. With festivities lasting for two weeks, the Chinese feasted with family, made sacrifices to the gods and used noisemakers to dispel evil spirits and bring good luck. The 10th-century Chinese invention of gunpowder made them the first culture to celebrate the New Year with fireworks.

... And Now

Today, celebrations often begin the night before with revelry and events on New Year's Eve and people staying up all night to usher in the New Year.

Eating, drinking and fireworks are common worldwide with countries highlighting a different symbolic food. For example, pork is a New Year's Eve mainstay in Portugal, Hungary and Austria because pigs represent prosperity in those cultures. In Italy, lentils are eaten because they resemble coins and may bring financial success. The Spanish eat twelve grapes at midnight to secure twelve happy months ahead of them. Ring-shaped cakes, symbolizing the full circle of the year, are enjoyed in Greece, Mexico and the Netherlands.

Scotland's New Year's celebration of Hogmanay is a rousing, all-night festivity of eating, drinking and music. In their tradition of "first-footing," people bearing good wishes and shortcake visit friends and family just after midnight. (And it's considered especially lucky if the first person to cross your threshold after midnight is a tall, dark and handsome man!)

Singing the Scottish ballad "Auld Lang Syne" is common in English-speaking countries. First published by poet Robert Burns in 1796, the song became popularly associated with New Year's in 1929 when bandleader Guy Lombardo played it at midnight at a New Year's Eve party in New York's Roosevelt Hotel.

In Japan, Oshogatsu is the year's most important holiday. People host "forget-the-year" parties in December and scrub their houses clean as a symbol of renewal. At midnight, Buddhist temples strike their gongs 108 times to rid themselves of the 108 human weaknesses. New Year's Day is a time of joy, relaxation and gifts for the children.

DID YOU KNOW?

- The current Times Square ball weighs over 11,000 pounds, measures twelve feet in diameter and is comprised of 2,688 Waterford Crystals and 32,000 LED lights.

- The Pasadena Rose Parade features 18 million flowers on its floats.

- About 45% of Americans make New Year's resolutions. Only 25% keep those resolutions longer than one week.

- According to legend, Buddha asked all the animals to meet him on Chinese New Year. Twelve showed up, and he named a year after each one (rat, ox, tiger, rabbit, dragon, snake, horse, sheep, monkey, rooster, dog and pig).

In America, the dropping of the ball at midnight in New York City has been a tradition since 1907 when *The New York Times* owner thought to have an illuminated, 700-pound iron-

and-wood ball lowered from the flagpole in Times Square. Today millions of people flock to world-famous locations including New York's Times Square, London's Trafalgar Square and Sydney Harbour to ring in the New Year with music, crowds and fireworks.

The first Rose Bowl game was played on January 1, 1902, which started a tradition of college football on New Year's Day. Popular parades include Pasadena's Tournament of Roses and Philadelphia's Mummers' Parade.

A Day of New Beginnings

While the Western New Year is celebrated on January 1, some cultures still follow the lunar calendar. Rosh Hashanah marks the Jewish New Year, usually in September or October, as a holy religious observance and a time of introspection. Muharram is the first month of the Islamic year, a sacred time that involves fasting and mourning. The Chinese New Year is celebrated for 15 days in late January to February with a Festival of Lanterns and a traditional dragon dance.

Wherever and whenever you celebrate it, the spirit is the same: starting anew.

Simple Tips for Greening New Year's

DECORATION

The key to eco-friendly decoration is moving away from disposable items whenever possible. By using the same décor every year, you'll save yourself both money and time running to the store for last-minute items.

- If you're hosting a party, decorate with fresh winter greenery just as ancient cultures did. Keep the Christmas tree up or trim some of its branches for use as boughs along the mantel, the windowsills or as table centerpieces. Let nature set the tone: fill glass bowls or vases with pinecones, nuts and bright red cranberries.

- Use fabric tablecloths and cloth napkins with your own tableware. If you'd rather not begin the new year washing dishes, use an eco-friendly brand of paper plates.

- Remember when people banged pots and pans to make a lot of noise? That's a DIY solution worth bringing back to replace plastic noisemakers. (And the kids will love it!) Alternatively, make noise by playing musical instruments, ringing bells or striking a Tibetan singing bowl. Part of the New Year's Eve buildup can revolve around activities where kids make their own noisemakers by recycling stuff you have around the house such as dried beans in a painted cardboard tube or nuts inside a tin can.

- Swap the store-bought party hats in favor of homemade ones—another great craft project for the kids. Have them create a New Year's party hat that will be brought out annually, perhaps with some new embellishment added on to it every year.

- Create atmosphere indoors with eco-friendly candles or by stringing LED lights around the party space. Outdoors, a beautiful alternative is the floating paper lantern, reminiscent of that scene in the Disney movie *Tangled*. I set off a few of these lanterns with friends for my 40th birthday. On a larger scale, my town disperses paper lanterns over the water during a Fall Equinox celebration. Made of bamboo and rice paper, the lanterns are 100% biodegradable. Releasing some of those into the sky makes for an interactive gathering and a festive display.

ACTIVITIES

- New Year's Eve is often about hitting the town. Plan to take public transportation, walk or carpool to your party or event. Some towns even promote this by offering free bus service to their city events, so check out your options. Buses, which emit 80% less carbon monoxide than the average car, can carry the equivalent of 60 car-loads of people. Walking or carpooling with a designated driver has the added advantage of allowing you to imbibe without worry.

TOP 5 POPULAR AMERICAN NEW YEAR'S RESOLUTIONS

- Lose weight
- Get organized
- Save more money
- Eat healthier and exercise
- Quit smoking

- Looking for someone to celebrate with? Try sites like Green Singles or Planet Earth Singles to add an eco flavor to your romance.

- Families can intersperse time around the television with time around an outdoor bonfire singing "Auld Lang Syne," sharing resolutions with each other or dancing to a mix of New Year-themed songs.

- Harken back to the Scottish tradition of first-footing, and call on your neighbors just after midnight. Make it a walking parade of your neighborhood bearing food and New Year's wishes at each house.

- Commit to some green resolutions alongside your typical ones. Make this the year you reduce your carbon footprint, volunteer with an environmental organization or invest in a hybrid car. Focusing on the positive aspects of a resolution may help you keep it longer. Instead of losing weight, pledge to buy more organic health foods or ride your bike to work. If you plan to quit smoking, donate the extra money to an eco charity that speaks to you.

- Kids can join in the fun by thinking of ways to go green in the coming year. Make a list of twelve green goals to move toward as a family—one for every month. Post it in a central location and have the kids add checkmarks or stickers for every related eco action they make each month.

FOOD AND DRINK

- **A Few Words on Wine** You can be eco-friendly with your New Year's drinks by choosing organic champagne, wine, beer or liquor. 100% organic wine contains no pesticides or added sulfites, which may reduce your New Year's Day headache. It also supports organic farmers whose farming methods conserve water and prevent soil erosion.

  You may have heard of biodynamic, or BD, wine. These wines are grown 100% organic in an approach that takes a whole-picture view of the growing process. For example, biodynamic farmers may plan their growing season by the phases of the moon or mix the manure of a lactating cow with water to fertilize their fields. While it may sound a bit kooky, biodynamic wines are known to taste better because of the deeper sense of place within them.

  Still, one of the greenest ways to drink (whether it's organic or not) is to buy locally from a nearby brewery or vineyard. By supporting local businesses, you boost the local economy and reduce pollution from shipping.

- Recycle your bottles. (Recycling just one glass bottle saves enough energy to power a CFL light bulb for eight hours!) You can even recycle wine corks at your local Whole Foods Market.

- Fight New Year's Day hangovers with peppermint tea (therapeutic for nausea and stomach problems); coconut water and bananas (both contain potassium for feeling better fast); or free-range eggs (the cysteine breaks down toxins in the liver).

GIFTS

Gift-giving was more popular on New Year's in earlier times, however it is still commonplace to bring food when visiting friends and family. Imitate the Romans and bring a fig and honey dessert or else share from your holiday bounty.

Out-of-the-Box Celebration Ideas

The essence of New Year's is beginnings and renewal. That's a theme you can honor in a variety of ways, without noisemakers or champagne, if you prefer.

- Get outdoors with friends and family for a winter hike… or a plunge in the local waters if you're Polar Bear inclined. Spending time outside on the first day of the new year (especially following a night of revelry or excess) feels wonderfully rejuvenating. America's state parks have started a tradition of First Day Hikes for January 1. Find or organize a hike in your area.

- Start the new year with a body cleanse. After the gluttony of the winter holidays, it feels good to rid the body of toxins, and it gives you a lighter start to the new year. Kids can do their own version of a cleanse by eliminating processed foods or sugars from their diet. A week or two will likely spark a difference in their eating habits.

- Even ancient cultures used New Year's Day to sweep out the old. Make January 1 a day of winter cleaning: open windows to let in fresh air and tackle a project you've been putting off whether it's that hallway closet or an area in the attic. Have the kids go through their toys and donate ones they rarely use (this also balances out the new ones they've just received). Afterwards, burn sage, sandalwood or rosemary incense to cleanse and purify a space.

- Along with making green resolutions, plan a year of eco activities. Mark the family calendar for Earth Day, Arbor Day, all the solstices and equinoxes, and then consider how you want to honor them. (See page 89 for a list of earth-friendly holidays by month.) Will you hike at a different park or wildlife refuge each time? Want to purchase a fruit tree to plant on Arbor Day? Do the research ahead of time. Plan ahead for making eco crafts.

Chapter 2:
Valentine's Day

History and Meaning

Valentine's Day, with its mix of Christian and pagan elements, has a history steeped in violence and fertility.

It all started with those hedonistic ancient Romans. In mid-February they celebrated Lupercalia, a fertility festival honoring Lupercus (Roman god of shepherds) and Faunus (Roman god of agriculture). The festival was a young man's rite of passage and consisted of male youths running through town gently slapping women and crops with pieces of sacrificial goat skin. The Romans believed this would enhance fertility for the coming year.

This general rowdiness was followed by a lottery in which all the town's willing young women put their names into an urn. Each man selected a name and the respective woman became his companion for the upcoming year. The partnerships often ended in marriage.

In an effort to "Christianize" these pagan traditions, Pope Gelasius outlawed the Lupercalia festival in 496 A.D. but retained the lottery aspect of the ritual. Only now instead of women's names in the urn, there were names of saints. Both men and women drew a name and, for the next year, were expected to imitate the life of the selected saint.

Who Was St. Valentine?

While the official history of St. Valentine remains murky, the most popular legend revolves around a priest who lived in Rome during the third century A.D. This was during the rule of Emperor Claudius II, who issued an edict forbidding young men to marry because he believed it would distract them from being good soldiers.

Valentine disagreed with the Emperor's views and continued to perform marriages in secret. It wasn't long before Claudius discovered this and threw him into prison.

According to legend, Valentine either fell in love with his jailer's daughter or healed her from blindness, and he wrote her letters signed "from your Valentine." He was subsequently beheaded on—you guessed it—February 14.

A few centuries later, St. Valentine was chosen to replace the pagan Lupercalia gods and represent the new Christian feast day. Pope Gelasius declared February 14 as St. Valentine's Day.

A Day of Love

However, it was still several centuries before Valentine's Day was widely celebrated as a romantic holiday. In some European countries, mid-February was long believed to be the time when birds chose their mates. With his tragi-romantic story, St. Valentine rose in popularity during the Middle Ages, and people began offering Valentine greetings to one another.

Geoffrey Chaucer is credited with linking the holiday to romance in his 1381 poem "The Parliament of Fowls" written to commemorate the engagement of England's Richard II and Anne of Bohemia.

DID YOU KNOW?

- Approximately 150 million Valentine's Day cards are exchanged every year, the second-highest holiday after Christmas.

- About 3% of pet owners give Valentines to their pets.

- The first Valentine's Day candy box of chocolates was produced by Richard Cadbury in the Victorian era.

- The oldest surviving love poem was written on a clay tablet from Sumeria around 3500 BC.

By the 18th century, Brits from all social classes were exchanging small gifts and handmade Valentines as a safe way to express one's true feelings. Handmade cards of lace and ribbon became popular, although cards weren't mass-produced until the 1840s when an American college graduate named Esther Howland started selling them. Her idea blossomed into a business—the New England Valentine Company—that popularized the Valentine greeting tradition in America. And that's how we swapped goat hides for greeting cards.

Today Valentine's Day is celebrated in the United States, the United Kingdom, France, Canada, Mexico, Australia, Denmark, Italy and Japan.

Simple Tips *for* Greening Valentine's Day

DECORATION

- **Conscious Candles** Set the ambiance for a romantic evening with clean-burning candles made of soy or beeswax. What's wrong with regular candles? They are typically made of paraffin (a by-product of petroleum) and, when burned, they release carcinogens into the air and into your lungs. Not very romantic, is it? Paraffin candles add to indoor pollution with their excess soot and smoke. Plus the chemical "fragrances" can lead to allergies, asthma and other health problems. Candles from other countries or ones made before 2003 likely contain lead-cored wicks. Do your kids a favor and ditch those.

  Eco candles made from beeswax or 100% soy are easy to find these days. They're non-toxic and last much longer, which makes up for their higher price. Beeswax candles make a good choice for tablecloths because they are drip-less. And buying beeswax helps support the diminishing bee population.

  Making your own eco candles is a fun, family-friendly activity for older kids. Add essential oils for a natural scent. Rechargeable LED candles are another option. They provide low-cost, flickering ambience without worry about smoke or chemicals.

- Essential oils are a natural way to inspire a romantic mood. Jasmine, ylang ylang and sandalwood are three oils known for their aphrodisiac qualities. Mix them in a carrier oil for a massage, or use an essential oil burner or aromatherapy diffuser to release their scent into a room.

ACTIVITIES

- Eating dinner out is a perfectly good way to honor the day, but how about trying a restaurant that's certified green? That means it has been assessed for sustainable practices such as water and energy efficiency, waste reduction and the sourcing of local ingredients. Search the Green Restaurant Association's website for a certified place near you. If you choose a restaurant nearby, extend the time together by walking there hand in hand. Want to be super green? Bring along your own reusable containers for leftovers.

  You can also find sustainable food options at EatWell-Guide.org. Punch in your zip code for a list of butchers, bakers, restaurants, farmers and more.

- At home, the family can enjoy a Valentine's meal (and save energy) dining by candlelight. Or create a cozy atmosphere with a picnic by the fireplace. Develop the meal plan together to include a favorite dish for everyone, and cook it as a family.

- Valentine's gifts don't have to be things; experiences are often more memorable. Watch romantic movies with your significant other. Enjoy a couples massage. Make a mix of meaningful love songs on your iPod. Visit places of significance in your relationship (where you met, first kiss, etc.).

GIFTS

- **Greeting Cards** I appreciate the fact that a 19th-century female college graduate was the ingenuity behind today's billion-dollar greeting card industry. However, nearly 150 million Valentine's cards are bought each year—that's a lot of trees! How about showing the trees some love too? E-cards are an excellent alternative, and they're often free. Personal phone calls, especially to loved ones who don't often hear from you, can mean a lot more than a piece of paper. Or get really creative with a personalized video.

  Consider alternatives to those perforated Valentines kids exchange in school. Could they make their own unique cards—perhaps using recycled materials—instead of buying mass-produced ones in bulk? That's how the Valentine card began anyway, with handmade touches of ribbon and lace. Or make your Valentine greetings edible by doling out healthy muffins or homemade fortune cookies with a personal message inside. In lieu of candy at school, give out holiday pencils, stickers or temporary tattoos.

TOP 5 BENEFITS OF DARK CHOCOLATE (MINIMUM 70% CACAO)

- *Good for your skin* (The high level of antioxidants protects skin from UV rays.)
- *Good for your heart* (The flavenols relax arteries and improve blood flow.)
- *Good for your brain* (Theobromine in the cacao promotes mental clarity.)
- *Good for your hair* (Copper, zinc and iron promote cell renewal.)
- *Good for your diet* (Rich in fiber, iron, magnesium and manganese.)

- **Chocolate and Wine:** These are two of the most traditional, and delicious, Valentine's Day gifts.

    Chocolate can be heaven in your mouth, and it tastes even better when you know no forests or children were harmed in its production. The chocolate industry threatens ecosystems by clearing forests, using pesticides on its higher-yield, hybrid cacao plants and enslaving children workers. The solution? Seek out chocolate with one of these labels: USDA-Certified Organic (cocoa grown without pesticides on well-managed land), Fair Trade Certified (workers are fairly paid and treated) and Rainforest Alliance Certified (cocoa grown without pesticides, using policies that protect the workers and the environment).

- **Flowers** Flowers are a big seller on this holiday, especially roses. But did you know that those picture-perfect roses are typically imported from other countries where the doses of insecticides and other heavy chemicals are not regulated? Even American-grown flowers often contain pesticides. To be on the safe side of those chemicals, choose one of these option below.

    Purchase organically grown flowers online or scout local nurseries that grow flowers in their greenhouse. Of course, if you live in a climate where flowers grow year-round, you can create your own wildflower bouquet.

    A greener option would be to give your loved one something that will actually last more than a few days, such as a flowering houseplant or windowsill herb garden. Or combine the greeting card and flowers together with biodegradable seeded cards. Seeds are embedded into the paper, which composts away as the card blooms into flowers, herbs or vegetables.

Out-of-the-Box Celebration Ideas

The essence of Valentine's Day is love, but love doesn't come in a box. It's a feeling. It's a verb. It's an experience. And you may just love some of these ideas for alternative Valentine's celebrations.

- Love makes us happy. So why not spend the entire day focusing on things you love from your cozy flannel sheets to the perfect omelet to an hour curled up with a juicy novel. Turn off the news. Avoid those negative friends. For one day, just focus on the things you love, and see how much better you feel at the end of it. Get the whole family involved and use dinner time to discuss the things everyone loves most.

- Make the day a live-action Valentine by pointing out the things you love about others. Tell your partner how much you appreciate the morning coffee he prepares for you every day or let your child know how her goodbye hugs make you smile. Sincerely spoken words can have more impact than anything else.

- Elicit the original essence of Lupercalia and its focus on fertility by trying to conceive today. It doesn't have to be a child. You can give birth to a new business, a family vacation or a plan for this year's garden. Maybe it's a good day to add a pet to the family. Or plant a tree. Or start writing your memoirs.

- Adapt the Roman tradition of a lottery for your family. Not sure what to do for Valentine's Day? Have everyone write down their craziest ideas and put them into a bowl. Pull one out and follow it. Or use the lottery for something silly: choose characters to imitate, foods to cook, movies to watch, daring questions to answer.

- Explore the theme of love and relationships in your city. Philadelphians have Robert Indiana's LOVE sculpture to ponder. New Yorkers have their "I (heart) NY" T-shirts to wear. Parisians have the Pont des Arts or 'lover's bridge' to explore. Zagreb, Croatia has its Museum of Broken Relationships. What does your town have? Your library likely features local love stories or events—start there.

Chapter 3:
St. Patrick's Day

History *and* Meaning

St. Patrick's Day, now a global event, has been observed by the Irish as a religious holiday for over 1,000 years.

Who was St. Patrick?

The patron saint of Ireland, Patrick is surrounded by much myth. For one, the man was not even Irish. He was actually born in Britain (then under control by the Romans) to an aristocratic family during the 5th century. At the age of 16, Patrick was kidnapped and brought to Ireland as a slave to tend sheep; he managed to escape years later.

According to legend, Patrick heard voices—perhaps from God—inspiring him to spread Christianity among the pagan Irish. So Patrick himself was ordained as a priest before returning to Ireland where he spent 30 years building churches and preaching to an often tough and rowdy crowd. He made his lessons more palatable by merging aspects of Christianity with traditional Irish culture. For example, Patrick is credited with incorporating the sun (revered by the Irish as a powerful and healing symbol) onto a Christian cross to create the now familiar Celtic cross.

Patrick allegedly died on March 17, 461, yet it wasn't until the 1600s that the Irish began celebrating that day in his honor.

Stories around Patrick grew over the centuries until he was made a saint by popular acclaim for being the man who completely Christianized Ireland (this was before the Catholic Church had an official canonization process). It was common for a saint's death to be commemorated as his feast day, so March 17 became St. Patrick's Day.

As the holy day usually fell during the Catholic season of Lent, St. Patrick's Day was a celebratory exception when the Irish could eat meat. Irish families attended church in the morning and gathered together later for food, drink and dancing.

The holy day expanded into its modern form thanks to Irish American immigrants who used the day to reconnect with their roots.

Parades

The first recorded St. Patrick's Day parade occurred in the United States on March 17, 1762, when Irish soldiers serving in the English army marched through New York City as a way of connecting to their homeland. It was a collection of Irish societies that united to form the official New York St. Patrick's Day parade in 1848. Today it is the world's longest-running civilian parade and the largest in the United States with about three million participants and observers combined.

With the Great Potato Famine of 1845 causing large numbers of Irish to flee to America, the new citizens were seen as a powerful voting block nicknamed the "Green Machine." St. Patrick's Day parades evolved into political venues attended by hopeful candidates. Today, politicians from Ireland regularly travel abroad for special functions on March 17.

St. Patrick's Day Symbols

The **shamrock**, or three-leafed clover, is considered an important plant in Ireland. Traditionally used for medicinal purposes, the shamrock signified the rebirth of spring and later, under suppression from the English, it became a symbol of Irish nationalism. Legend says Patrick used the shamrock to explain the Christian concept of the Holy Trinity to the Irish.

Music has always been a central part of Irish culture and a way of passing on stories through the generations. The Irish clung to it even more when music was outlawed by the English under Queen Elizabeth's rule for inciting emotion and potential uprisings. Today, Irish music is central to many St. Patrick's Day parades and celebrations.

Legend credits St. Patrick for banishing all the **snakes** from Ireland. Actually, Ireland never had any snakes because the icy cold water surrounding the Emerald Isle keeps the animal from migrating there. The "evil" snake was used more as a metaphor for Patrick banishing paganism in favor of Christianity.

Leprechauns were always a part of ancient Celtic folklore. They existed alongside faeries as magical yet cranky little people known for their trickery and hidden treasure. Yet it is American culture that is responsible for associating the leprechaun with St. Patrick's Day through Walt Disney's 1959 release of the movie *Darby O'Gill & the Little People*. This cheerful portrayal of a leprechaun was quickly adopted as a fun American symbol for the Irish holiday.

The color **green** was likely another American add-on since it actually was considered unlucky in Ireland. The Irish believed green to be the favorite color of the faeries who might steal those children who wore too much of it. Blue was the color traditionally associated with St. Patrick.

DID YOU KNOW?

- On a normal day, about 5.5 million pints of Guinness are consumed around the world. On St. Patrick's Day, that number jumps to 13 million.

- About 650,000 babies born in the U.S. over the last century have been named Patrick.

- The New York City St. Patrick's Day parade covers 2.1 miles, showcases 150 bands and lasts nearly six hours.

- The St. Patrick's Day parade didn't appear in Ireland until the 1840s when Temperance organizations hoped the activity might distract the Irish from drinking. (It didn't.)

A Day of Good Cheer

Up until the 1970s in Ireland, St. Patrick's Day was observed as a simple religious holiday where families went to church, shared a big meal… and the pubs remained closed. It wasn't until 1995 when the government decided to use the holiday to spark tourism and showcase Irish culture. Now Dublin's annual St. Patrick's Festival is a weeklong event of parades, concerts and a fireworks display called Skyfest.

The holiday has largely lost its association with religion or politics or being of Irish descent. Today people observe St. Patrick's Day more as a day of good cheer. While celebrations are largest in the United States, Canada and Australia, countries such as Russia, China and Japan honor the day with their own parades and festivities.

Simple Tips for Greening St. Patrick's Day

DECORATION

- Even those who aren't Irish tend to wear green on St. Patrick's Day, and you can do it sustainably. Scour secondhand stores for green garments. (I always see barely worn "Kiss Me, I'm Irish" T-shirts at my local thrift store.) If you buy something new, choose natural materials like wool, silk or organic cotton.

- Party decoration can be inexpensive and easy. Simply gather all your houseplants (real or fake) together in one room for a lush, green atmosphere. Or bring together every green item you own from pillows and curtains to knickknacks and children's toys.

- All you really need to create atmosphere is a bit o' Irish music. Find a station on Pandora or start your own jam session. Know anyone who plays classic Irish instruments like the fiddle, flute or bodhran? Kids can play along with a tin penny whistle, a common Irish instrument.

ACTIVITIES

- Attend a local parade, and pitch in to help clean up afterwards. (Parades are notorious trash generators: New York's St. Patty's Day parade creates about 50 tons of trash!)

If there isn't a parade in your town, form your own with neighborhood families—it's energizing to get outside in March and breathe in the fresh air.

- Check out an Irish step dancing class or performance. Learn how to dance an Irish jig yourself.

- Host an afternoon of potato-themed crafts from the traditional potato stamp to battery powered LED clocks.

- Check out leprechaun stories from the library to discover the Irish legends behind these magical creatures. Watch *Darby O'Gill & the Little People* to see where the Americanized leprechaun came from.

FOOD AND DRINK

- Many Irish Americans dine on corned beef and cabbage for St. Patrick's Day, but only half of that dish harkens back to the Emerald Isle. Cabbage is a traditional Irish food, but corned beef is an American addition from New York City's Irish immigrants who borrowed the idea from their Jewish neighbors. They substituted corned beef for the traditional Irish bacon because it was cheaper.

- **Green Foods** As tempting as the holiday's "green" foods may be, it's best to avoid the unnaturally green-colored options. Those synthetic food dyes (FD&C Green No.3) are derived from petroleum and are associated with hyperactivity in children, cancer and allergic reactions. Though still legal in the U.S., these food dyes have been banned in Europe.

  Instead try celebrating St. Patty's Day with a green-themed dinner of real food. What can you create from cabbage, pesto, asparagus, kiwi, grapes or avocado? Get the kids involved in making spinach pasta or pistachio ice cream. Better yet, eat green by shopping for local and organic foods.

- **A Bit o' Brew** Before the 19th century, all beer was organic. And it tasted better. The explosion of the pesticide and chemical industries has resulted in traces of toxins in our beer, our bodies, our land and groundwater. Buying organic beer avoids such toxins and comes with its own health benefits. Organic hops and barley are a good source of B6 and anti-inflammatory bioflavonoids—both are better absorbed by your body without toxins present. As an added bonus, organic hops have been linked to cancer prevention. There's something to toast!

Other green drinking alternatives include buying locally made brews, brewing your own beer or supporting eco-friendly beer companies. Colorado's New Belgium Brewery (Fat Tire beer) was the nation's first wind-powered brewery, and Sierra Nevada Brewery uses solar panels, hydrogen fuel cells and trucks powered on 100% vegetable oil waste.

TOP 5 POPULAR IRISH PHRASES

- *Erin go Bragh* (Ireland forever)
- *Cead Mile Fáilte* (A hundred thousand welcomes)
- *May the road rise to meet you* (May success be with you)
- *Sláinte!* (To your health!)
- *How's the craic?* (How are you?)

Out-of-the-Box Celebration Ideas

Outside of its religious origins, the essence of St. Patrick's Day is about cultural pride and good cheer.

- If you're Irish, spend the day learning more about your ancestry and culture. Can you trace your Irish family tree? Are there any family songs or stories that have been passed down? Learn Irish Gaelic words and phrases by playing a dictionary-style game where players make up definitions and have to guess which meaning is actually true.

- Even if you're not Irish, you can make March 17 a day of personal pride. Have everyone in your family make lists of what they love most about themselves. Each person wears her favorite color and makes a flag representing her true self. Then get together and have a parade to exhibit everyone's uniqueness.

- Take St. Patrick's mission of conversion and convert your family to a greener lifestyle. Make March 17 a day for incorporating a few green actions each year. Switch all your bulbs to CFLs and LEDs. Start a vegetable garden. Start a compost bin. Replace paper towels with cloth rags. Go vegetarian one day each week.

- Immerse yourself in the world of magical Celtic folklore: build fairy houses outside, read about pookas and kelpies, or put on a puppet show of leprechauns crafted from old socks.

Chapter 4:
Easter, Passover and Spring Festivals

History and Meaning

Easter, considered the most important Christian holiday, and Passover, perhaps the Jewish religion's most sacred holiday, overlap in their history and are both celebrated in early spring.

To Christians, Easter is a day that celebrates the resurrection of Jesus three days after his crucifixion and death. Lent, meant to be a time of reflection and penance, is the 40-day period leading up to Easter Sunday. It represents the 40 days Jesus spent alone in the wilderness before beginning his mission. Jesus' crucifixion occurred after he celebrated Passover in Jerusalem.

Passover (*Pesach* in Hebrew) is a weeklong event that commemorates Moses leading the Israelites' out of Egyptian slavery and into a 40-year trek through the Sinai desert to their ancestral home. The holiday is named because an angel sent to slay firstborn sons "passed over" the marked homes of the Jews.

While Christians at one time observed Easter every Sunday, by the third century it was designated to one day near the Jewish Passover, from which many Easter rituals were taken. The date changes each year, but the calculation is the same. Western Christians celebrate Easter on the first Sunday following the full moon after the spring equinox—which typically falls between the end of March and the end of April. (Eastern Orthodox Christians do the same, except they use the Julian calendar so the dates often do not match.)

Easter shares strong parallels with pagan symbols. Some even believe the name 'Easter' was derived from Eostre or Ostara, a Teutonic goddess of spring and fertility. She was honored around the vernal equinox and her sacred animal was the rabbit—which may explain those Easter bunny connections.

What Do Those Symbols Mean?

Easter Bunny In our modern-day American version of the holiday, the Easter Bunny has become as commercial as Santa Claus, delivering sugar-infested treats inside cheap plastic eggs. Where did this bunny come from? As a known symbol of fertility and spring, the rabbit was likely co-opted from pagan tradition.

In addition, legends about egg-laying rabbits were documented in the 17th century. One example is a story about an egg-laying hare named Osterhase that German immigrants brought to America in the 1700s. Children made nests for the Osterhase to lay his colorful eggs. Those nests eventually translated to baskets and the real eggs into chocolate ones.

Eggs An ancient symbol in many cultures, eggs represent new life. People once believed the Earth hatched from an egg, and eggs were often used in spring festivals of the early Romans and Egyptians. Christians use the egg to symbolize Jesus' resurrection from the tomb. A hard-boiled egg dipped in salt water represents new life in the Passover Seder.

Sources date the tradition of decorating Easter eggs back to medieval times when the food was forbidden during Lent. People decorated eggs during the period of fasting and enjoyed them on Easter as a prized gift. Hunts and rolls were two popular egg-related activities. Children in England and Germany, respectively, would roll eggs down hills on Easter morning and hunt for eggs hidden by Osterhase—both customs were brought to America.

Parades The origin of Easter parades may harken back to early European Christians who participated in a procession following Easter Mass. The popular New York City Easter Parade has its roots in the mid-19th century when folks attended church services and, afterward, strolled along Fifth Avenue to show off their fancy spring hats. The stroll became a tradition, and the Manhattan Easter Parade continues today along with Easter parades in other cities.

A Day of Rebirth

Both Easter and Passover celebrate a triumph over hardship (death and enslavement) just as pagan cultures celebrated spring as a triumph over the long, dark winter. Although the stories and traditions may differ across religions, the holiday is essentially about rebirth.

Today Easter is celebrated in different fashions around the world and under various names: Ostern in Germany, Pascua in Spain and Paques in France.

Spring Festivals Around the World

While the commercialized Easter may usher in spring in America, almost every culture has a way of celebrating the season. Hindus in India and Nepal celebrate *Holi*, the Festival of Colors, with bonfires and colored powder they toss at each other. Some countries celebrate spring as the beginning of their New Year, such as the Iranian *Nowruz*.

May Day, or *Beltane,* is celebrated in many countries on May 1 as the beginning of spring. The maypole dance has its roots in pagan history when European cultures danced around the pole to attract a fertile planting season. The pole

DID YOU KNOW?

- The first official White House Easter Egg Roll took place in 1878 under President Rutherford B. Hayes, although egg rolling on the grounds of the U.S. Capitol can be traced as far back as President Andrew Johnson.

- Around 90 million chocolate Easter bunnies, 16 billion jelly beans and five million marshmallow chicks and bunnies (a.k.a. Peeps) are produced for Easter.

- Coca-Cola makes a Kosher Coke for Passover that replaces the forbidden high fructose corn syrup with actual sugar.

- The world's largest matzo ball (unveiled at the 2010 Tucson Jewish Food Festival) weighed 488 pounds and contained 1,000 eggs, 125 pounds of matzo meal and 25 pounds of chicken fat.

(usually from a felled tree) is often viewed as a phallic symbol but may also have been the German way of honoring the trees they deemed sacred. The pagan association was transformed in Victorian England when the maypole dance became a celebration of young, virtuous maidens.

Today, the maypole is colorfully decorated and erected on the village green as part of springtime celebrations in many countries including Germany, Austria, Sweden, the United Kingdom and Italy (where it is more of a political tradition that involves putting a red flag in a treetop).

Simple Tips for Greening Spring Holidays

Incorporating green into your spring holidays is fairly easy with nature blooming all around you. Many of the plastic, disposable items used for this holiday can be replaced with real alternatives.

DECORATION

- *A Better Basket* If your kids already have plastic Easter baskets from previous holidays, it's better to reuse them annually rather than increase the overflowing landfills. However, if you're starting fresh, think outside the basket. See what containers from around the house you can repurpose for Easter treats. It might be a fancy box, a ceramic bowl, a fabric bag or a natural wicker basket. Or look online for Fair Trade baskets.

  A longstanding May Day tradition, handmade May baskets were often left on doorsteps with fresh flowers or treats inside. Add basket-making as a spring activity for the kids by making your own from paper scraps and wallpaper samples. Fill it with flowers, and surprise a neighbor.

- Layer your baskets with shredded paper, raffia or a colorful scarf instead of that hideous plastic grass we grew up with. The plastic stuff is very enticing—and very harmful—to pets if ingested. Alternatively, you can also grow your own wheatgrass at home and use that inside the containers.

- Household decoration is easy with fresh flowers. Plant bulbs the previous fall to have a springtime bloom of daffodils, tulips or crocuses. Perhaps you'll decide to invest in or create a fabric banner or garden flag to hang outside the house every year. Choose a design for every season and reuse the flags annually.

- Search online for "recycled crafts" and you'll find tons of ideas for the whole family from toilet paper roll Easter bunnies to Passover wine goblets of recycled plastic. While these kinds of decoration require an investment of time, they also provide your kids with something fun to do over school vacation.

ACTIVITIES

- Green the traditional egg hunt or egg roll by ditching the plastic eggs. Although reusing the eggs you already have is typically the most eco-friendly step, a 2008 report revealed that some plastic eggs are contaminated with lead paint. To be on the safe side, you may want to do something a bit different.

    Bypass the egg altogether and just hide the treats themselves (my mom used to do this). Decorate and use hardboiled, ceramic or wooden eggs for an egg roll. Check your local craft store for cardboard eggs that can be sliced open to store treats. If you're crafty, you can make egg-shaped holders from felt or yarn to contain a few treats.

- Honor ancient Eastern European egg-decorating traditions, often referred to by the Ukrainian term *pysanky*. You might find a local pysanky class or follow an online tutorial.

- Make your own chocolate. This way you know exactly what's going into it. Find recipes online that use everything from organic cocoa powder and coconut oil to agave and almond butter. Gluten-free options abound as well.

- Gather the neighborhood kids together for a spring maypole dance. You can make your own maypole using a large branch and colorful ribbons.

- Host a Family Movie Night of spring-themed films. Choose your theme: religious (*The Ten Commandments, Jesus Christ Superstar*); musical (*Easter Parade, State Fair*); youthful (*Hop, 'It's the Easter Beagle,' Charlie Brown*); or sporty, since it is also the start of baseball season (*Field of Dreams, The Sandlot*).

FOOD AND DRINK

- ***Eco Easter Eggs*** Buy eggs from your local farmer's market or look in the grocery store for eggs marked "Certified Humane" or "Animal Welfare Approved." This means the eggs come from happy chickens, and they usually taste better too! You can also search LocalHarvest.org for local eggs from chickens, ducks and geese. At the grocery store, consider the packaging; choose eggs in compostable cardboard containers over Styrofoam or plastic ones.

  As egg shells are extremely porous, what you dye them with matters. Purchase food-safe dyes or 100% organic versions.

  Another option is to make a fun, eco activity out of dyeing eggs with foods from your kitchen. Onions, berries, cabbage and turmeric can be transformed into beautiful colors. To make cool shapes or patterns on your egg, use a beeswax crayon to draw on the egg before dyeing, wrap the egg with twine for a striped pattern or experiment with making impressions of leaves and flowers.

- *A Sustainable Seder* Be thoughtful in selecting your Seder meal—horseradish, karpas, matzah and charoset ingredients can all be bought organic. Make them truly local by growing your own parsley, celery or onion for the karpas. Opt for grass-fed lamb and brisket. Kosher wine is available in organic varieties. Serve it all on reusable dinnerware.

  When ridding your home of chametz, don't just toss the food away. Pass the bread, oats, barley, etc. to non-Jewish neighbors, share it with the squirrels and birds or donate it to a local food pantry.

- *Candy with a Conscience* When it comes to chocolate, focus on quality over quantity. Chocolate labeled "Fair Trade Certified" or "Rainforest Alliance Certified" ensures that your holiday bunnies weren't made at the expense of others. You can find such chocolate online along with gluten-free and peanut-free candy options.

  You might enjoy the fun (and the ingredient control) of making your own candy. Turn to Pinterest for homemade recipes for "Peeps," gummy candy or jelly beans.

  Make your store-bought candy choices based on eliminating excess packaging. This might mean choosing the chocolate egg wrapped in simple aluminum foil over the one encased in plastic and cardboard.

GIFTS

- In lieu of a sugar-infested holiday, consider non-candy treats that shout "springtime" such as finger paints, sidewalk chalk and bubbles. My daughter's first spring basket contained a book, a pair of sandals and a stuffed animal, and she loved it. Some other natural gift ideas include kids' gardening tools and seeds, wood toys, beeswax crayons, play silks and cloth puppets.

- Give a springtime experience instead of stuff. A trip to a farm or children's museum, tickets to a play or baseball game, or a day at an amusement park.

- As tempting as it can be, do not buy your kids a bunny for Easter unless you're serious about one as a long-term pet. The House Rabbit Society rescues too many "disposable" bunnies just after Easter each year. My family has cared for several bunnies over the years, and they require as much attention as a dog or cat. Rabbits should not be seen as a cute, quick Easter gift. If you want to give a bunny to someone, donate to a needy family through Heifer.org.

Out-of-the-Box Celebration Ideas

The essence of Easter, Passover and spring is rebirth. Days grow longer. Buds bloom. Baby animals are born. It's a time of new beginnings and transitions. It's definitely a time for being outdoors.

- Turn over fresh earth for a flower or vegetable garden. Jump into the ocean in a springtime version of the Polar Bear Club. Visit a farm to see baby animals being born. Put together a parade for the neighborhood. Have the kids construct their own "Easter bonnets" from recycled materials and march through the streets. Enjoy a family walk looking for signs of spring.

- Since this is the time of new beginnings, you may decide to create yearly resolutions now instead of January. What areas of your life require transformation? Is it time to adopt a new attitude toward your boss? To switch some stale roles with your partner (he cleans the bathroom and you mow the lawn)? While the focus shouldn't be on perfection, it can be fun to reimagine parts of yourself. Access the bold/flirty/carefree/patient qualities in yourself that you usually admire in others.

- After winter, spring is about bursts of color, as exemplified in the Indian festival of Holi. Make your spring a feast of colors. Get out the chalk and draw murals on your driveway. Hang banners of silks and fabrics. Prepare a feast in colors of the rainbow from chocolate-dipped strawberries and plump, purple grapes to balsamic-dressed field greens and spaghetti squash.

TOP 5 ESSENTIAL OILS FOR SPRING CLEANING

- *Tea Tree:* Its natural disinfectant properties work well against mold and mildew.

- *Lemon:* Brightens whites, removes stains and cuts through grease and grime.

- *Peppermint:* This powerful antibacterial agent acts as a pest deterrent and leaves a fresh scent.

- *Sweet Orange:* A natural antiseptic and insecticide, it's excellent for degreasing and wood polishing.

- *Rosemary:* An antibacterial and disinfectant with excellent deodorizing capabilities, it was often used during ancient cleansing rituals.

- Spring cleaning is a natural rite for this time of year (and it's also a part of the Passover ritual) because it breathes new life into your home. Our rooms and possessions all vibrate with energy, which can become stale from clutter or neglect. Regular clearing can "unstick" old energy. Open windows to let fresh air circulate. Donate things you don't need anymore. Use non-toxic cleaning ingredients like vinegar and baking soda. Simply rearranging furniture can provide a whole new look and feel to a space.

Chapter 5:
Independence Day

History and Meaning

The Fourth of July is a commemoration of America's declaration of independence from Great Britain.

In 1775 the Revolutionary War broke out as American colonists butted heads with the British monarchy over certain issues such as increased taxation, under-representation in Parliament and the unwanted presence of the British Army in the colonies. One year later, the Continental Congress (the government of the 13 colonies) met in Philadelphia to discuss the possibility of separating from Great Britain.

A five-man committee that included Thomas Jefferson, Benjamin Franklin and John Adams was appointed to draft a document presenting the case for independence. Congress reconvened and voted almost unanimously for separation from Great Britain. Although the vote was made two days earlier, July 4, 1776 was the day when the Continental Congress officially adopted the Declaration of Independence. Even then, it wasn't actually signed until August!

TOP 5 AMERICAN EVENTS THAT OCCURRED ON JULY 4

- 1826 – Both John Adams and Thomas Jefferson die on this 50th anniversary of the adoption of the Declaration of Independence.

- 1827 - New York State frees its slaves.

- 1884 – The formal presentation of the Statue of Liberty takes place in the Gauthier workshop in Paris.

- 1930 – Gutzon Borgium's 60-foot face of George Washington is carved onto Mount Rushmore in Keystone, South Dakota.

- 1980 – Throughout the country, the Fourth is observed amid somber recognition of the 53 American citizens held hostage in Iran; residents in Cleveland plant 53 trees in the hostages' memory.

Just days after the Fourth, Americans began celebrating with public readings of the Declaration and mock funerals for King George III. The first official commemoration of Independence Day was held in Philadelphia on July 4, 1777, even though the Revolutionary War continued until 1783. Festivities included parades, bonfires, music and cannon firings. In 1781,

Massachusetts became the first state to make July 4th an official state holiday.

Independence Day emitted a strong political atmosphere over the next century, and celebrations often revolved around highlighting the latest leaders and creating unity among political parties. Observations of the day increased in popularity after America's victory over Great Britain in the War of 1812. Towns across the country began celebrating the summertime holiday with picnics, contests, military displays and fireworks. It was in 1870 when the United States Congress made July 4th a national holiday, becoming a paid holiday for federal employees in 1941.

Today the Fourth of July is still celebrated across the United States with cookouts, parades and fireworks. Philadelphia holds one of the biggest celebrations with reenactments at Independence Hall and the country's "largest free concert" and fireworks display over the Museum of Art. In Boston, the USS John F. Kennedy sails into Boston Harbor, and the Boston Pops Orchestra plays a televised concert of American music.

A Day of Independence

Many countries have their own Independence Days celebrated with similar festivities. Perhaps the most well known is the French Bastille Day (July 14) marked by fireworks, dance parties and the pardoning of some prisoners.

September is a big month for these Latin countries that honor their independence with parades, music and bullfights: Brazil on September 7, Chile on September 18, and Mexico on September 16 (not Cinco de Mayo, which is more of an American celebration of Mexican culture).

South Africa honors their independence from Britain—and the restoration of human rights after apartheid—on April 27. India celebrates the Fifteenth of August as their national holiday with parades, songs and a competitive tradition of kite flying.

Simple Tips for Greening Independence Day

DECORATION

On this patriotic day, decoration can be as simple as flying the American flag. If you want to do it up with additional red, white and blue décor, opt for items that can be reused from year to year.

- Show your colors from Memorial Day through Labor Day by planting garden beds of red (roses), white (shasta daisies) and blue (hydrangea). Or create centerpieces of red (fresh berries), white (bananas) and blue (more berries) fruits in glass bowls.

- Get the kids involved in making bunting from fabric scraps. Nix the mylar balloons in favor of 100% latex, which is a natural product of rubber tree sap and, therefore, biodegradable.

- Even crepe paper comes in eco options now. For a more stylish look, decorate outside with strings of colorful LED lights or solar lanterns that let the sun do the work.

- Keep bugs away with eco-friendly citronella candles or essential oil blends of geranium, rosemary, peppermint or lavender. Plan the party area of your yard ahead of time with bugs in mind. Landscape the area with plants that naturally deter mosquitoes, such as citronella (a perennial grass), marigolds, lemon balm and catnip.

- What about those popular glow sticks kids love? They're filled with an oily liquid called dibutyl phthalate. And while the National Capital Poison Center says the chemical is not deadly, it is a substance used to manufacture glues, nail polish, plastics, printing inks and more—not something I'd like my child to accidentally swallow or have splash in her eyes when a cheap glow stick breaks.

Plus glow sticks are a single-use item, thousands of which permeate our landfills. Search online for "glow stick alternative" and you'll find LED-powered flashlights and battery-powered glow sticks.

ACTIVITIES

- **Facts about Fireworks** Unfortunately, the fireworks that light up the nighttime sky aren't very good for the earth or your health. They pollute the air with smoke and produce a shower of toxic chemicals and heavy metals, including radioactive barium, arsenic, lead and thyroid-disrupting perchlorates. They also cause more fires in the U.S. than any other day of the year. Not much of a celebration, is it?

    Investigate perchlorate-free fireworks. Some companies are exploring this less toxic technology that's often used in theme parks and larger venues. While it may still be too pricey for individual use, you can see if your local town or community is willing to invest in perchlorate-free fireworks. Laser shows are another fireworks alternative.

    At home, you can set off a beautiful and silent display of biodegradable floating lanterns, as mentioned in Chapter 1 for New Year's. Since many young children are scared of the noise from fireworks, this is an earth- and kid-friendly alternative.

- If you're hosting a party, plan one around using the least amount of energy. On a hot day, host an evening soiree when it's naturally cooler. During the daytime, choose a shady location in your backyard or at a local park. Inside, use fans instead of air conditioning.

Rather than running hoses or sprinklers (which can waste 265 gallons of water per hour—more than the average U.S. household uses daily), let the kids cool off with homemade popsicles or a dip in a nearby lake. Toss ice cubes down their shirts, or keep washcloths in the freezer—they feel great around your neck!

- Encourage recycling by placing bins where guests can easily locate them. Instead of individual water bottles, fill glass pitchers with water, lemonade or iced tea. Got a lot of beer drinkers? A mini keg might be more cost-efficient than purchasing bottles or cans, and it definitely reduces the packaging waste.

FOOD AND DRINK

- Hot dogs, hamburgers, potato salad, cole slaw, corn on the cob, watermelon... none of these foods were on the menu for those early Independence Days. Rather, John Adams and friends feasted on turtle soup, peas and New England poached salmon with egg sauce. Say what?

    Turtle soup, especially, was a favorite as turtle catching was a regular summertime sport. Concern for turtle preservation eventually made the soup passé, and in the early 1800s, roasted pig (popular with New York immigrants) became the new dish for July 4th picnics. While hamburgers and hot dogs eventually replaced roasted pig, the tradition of cooking outside is what really carried through the centuries.

    Back then, people ate whatever was readily available locally, and you can do the same. Visit your farmers market for the freshest fruits and veggies to share, and cook up some creative dishes.

If burgers are on your menu, opt for turkey or chicken instead of beef because cows carve out a much larger carbon footprint than those birds do. Vegetarian burgers are even greener, and some of the ones available today are quite tasty and filling.

* **Pick Your Plates** For your picnic, forgo the disposable plates for eco-friendly options that won't break the budget. Comb summer yard sales and thrift stores for a funky collection of glasses and plates that you use strictly for parties. If you don't have the storage space for that, there are biodegradable options.

Bamboo-made BAMBU plates are intended for single-use but often last longer. Preserve offers 100% recycled plastic plates and EATware makes compostable ones. Treecycle has all sorts of compostable and biodegradable cups, plates and bowls made from sugar cane.

Renting glasses and tableware is a pricier option, but it may serve you well for large events.

DID YOU KNOW?

* About 60 million Americans fire up the grill each 4th of July—that's enough energy to power the town of Flagstaff, Arizona for one year!

* 97% of U.S. fireworks and 87% of U.S. flags are imported from China.

* Benjamin Franklin was displeased with the selection of the bald eagle as the national bird, describing the animal as "...a Bird of bad moral character." He considered the turkey a more respectable symbol.

- As for grilling, studies have shown that gas grills are the most eco-friendly option. The liquefied petroleum gas burns more efficiently and releases half the amount of carbon emissions compared to asthma-inducing charcoal, which also emits more soot and VOCs. If you prefer charcoal, you can grill greener with sustainably produced charcoal certified by the Forestry Stewardship Council. Some brands include Wicked Good Charcoal and Big Green Egg. Buying sustainably harvested charcoal means less deforestation, fewer emissions and healthier grilled food.

  You can also try a solar cooker that harnesses the sun's energy to cook your food without a trace of noxious gases.

Out-of-the-Box Celebration Ideas

The essence of Independence Day is, well, independence. Proclaim freedom from tradition by celebrating the Fourth in your own unique way.

- The dictionary defines *independence* as "freedom from the control, influence, support, aid, or the like, of others." So make July 4th a day to yourself unhampered by schedules, clocks and the demands of others. Escape into nature. Drive aimlessly on a solo adventure. Lie around and read all day. Arrange a playdate for yourself. Do whatever your heart desires.

- Create a Yes Day for your kids by saying "yes" to whatever they ask for—with regards to safety, of course. Or grant them freedom for an entire day. Let them choose their own meals, their outfits, the family activities, whether or not they even want to get out of bed.

- Since countries use Independence Day to focus on their national history, perhaps you want to focus on your family history. If you haven't a clue to who your ancestors are beyond your own grandparents, this could be a fun introduction to your family tree. Begin online at FamilySearch.com to search genealogical records for free. If you already have boxes of old photos and keepsakes, make a family activity of organizing them into a scrapbook of memories.

- On the ecological front, declare your independence from oil or toxins by making a green change in favor of alternative transportation or organic skin care products.

- As a family, you could focus on those who are not free. Educate your kids about some current global issues and volunteer for an organization like Amnesty International. Rescue a pet from a shelter, or donate your time there. Make lists of everything you appreciate about your own personal freedom.

Chapter 6:
Halloween

History *and* Meaning

Halloween is considered one of the world's oldest holidays—
its origins harken back to the ancient Celtic festival of Samhain
(pronounced *sow-een* or *sow-in*).

Samhain was celebrated on October 31, the night marking
the end of the harvest season and the beginning of the Celtic
New Year and a long, dark winter. The Celts believed it to be
a magical night when the ghosts of the newly dead (as well as
fairies, witches and demons) mingled with the living during
their travels to the otherworld. People lit huge bonfires and
sacrificed animals and crops to aid the dead in their journey
and to keep them from wreaking havoc on those still living.

Centuries later, the Catholic Church tried to transform the pagan Samhain by honoring the dead with two holy days: All Saints Day on November 1 and All Souls Day on November 2. European celebrations remained similar—bonfires, parades and costumes—although the wandering dead spirits took on a slightly more evil connotation. Folks tried to appease these spirits with food and drink.

Why the name Halloween? All Saints Day was also known as All Hallows (*hallowed* meaning 'holy'). The night before— October 31, or All Hallows Eve—eventually translated into Halloween.

Halloween was slow to spread in North America. In colonial times, harvest celebrations or "play parties" involved singing, dancing, fortune-telling, ghost stories and general mischief-making. The 19th century influx of Irish immigrants helped to popularize Halloween with their own traditions.

The Origin of Halloween Traditions

Precursors to **trick-or-treating** go back to the ancient Celts who sometimes disguised themselves in animal skins to ward off evil spirits during Samhain. In Medieval times, there arose the custom of "mumming" where people dressed up like the ghosts, fairies and witches they feared and performed antics in exchange for food and drink.

After Christianity took hold of Europe, mumming was transformed into the practice of "going a-souling." During All Souls Day parades in England, the poor would beg for food, specifically a pastry known as a "soul cake." The beggars would receive the sweets in exchange for promising to pray for the giver's deceased family members.

Then there is Guy Fawkes Night, or Bonfire Night, in Britain. In 1605 Guy Fawkes led a Catholic conspiracy to overthrow

King James I. Fawkes' subsequent execution was celebrated annually with bonfires as children donned masks and roamed the streets begging for pennies.

English, Irish and Scottish immigrants brought all these customs to America where they merged into our modern-day trick-or-treating. The custom boomed in the 1950s when sugar was no longer rationed by war, suburbia made it safe for kids to wander the streets at night, and television launched national advertising campaigns for candy.

Carving pumpkins harkens back to Samhain when the Celts carved harvest vegetables and used them to carry the embers from the sacred bonfire back to their homes. In Ireland and Scotland, people carved scary faces into turnips, beets and potatoes to frighten away evil spirits, including a legendary one named Stingy Jack, from which the term "Jack of the Lantern" evolved.

Bobbing for apples may have been derived from the Roman festival of Pomona (the goddess of fruit and trees), which mingled with Samhain when the Romans conquered the Celts. Apples were plentiful at harvest time and were often used in fortune telling.

DID YOU KNOW?

- According to the National Retail Federation, Americans spend upwards of $5 billion on the spooky celebration.
- New York City is known for its famous ghosts who include the likes of Mark Twain, Dylan Thomas, Peter Stuyvesant and Aaron Burr.

A Day of the Dead

Today Halloween is celebrated "American style" in the United States, Canada, France, Italy and Germany. Here it has become less about the supernatural and more of a children's holiday of parades, candy and costumes.

Mexico, Latin America and Spain celebrate *Dia de los Muertos*, a Day of the Dead festival from October 31 to November 2 when families gather for parties and to reunite with the spirits of their dead relatives.

In Eastern Europe, All Saints Day is observed as a somber occasion of prayer and visiting cemeteries. In the United Kingdom, celebrations range from Celtic bonfires, pranks and games in Ireland to bonfires and fireworks for Guy Fawkes Day in England.

Simple Tips *for* Greening Halloween

DECORATION

As in spring, the natural plants and foods of the season often make the easiest and most beautiful décor.

- Decorate with fall fruits and vegetables (pumpkins, gourds, corn, etc.) to honor the season's harvest as the Celts did. Colorful, seasonal mums brighten the house inside and out. Bales of straw can decorate your yard and can then be used to cover your garden beds for winter.

- If you already have paper and plastic Halloween décor, just use them again every year. The more worn they become, the scarier they'll look! Otherwise, get creative using materials you already have. Build a skeleton from twigs and branches painted white. Stuff fallen leaves into old clothes for scarecrows or dead bodies. Cut out creepy silhouettes for your windows from scrap fabric or newspaper. Reuse old bedsheets to make flying ghosts and witches.

• Add atmosphere and save energy by keeping the house dark except for candles or LED string lights.

• **Creative Costuming** Although an easy solution, those cheap, store-bought costumes are rarely made with natural fabrics and could be teeming with harmful chemicals such as arsenic, lead, mercury and volatile organic compounds (VOCs). You can save worry and money by seeking out a neighborhood costume swap; many are held nationwide on October's National Costume Swap Day. If there isn't a swap in your area, host one yourself. You probably know plenty of parents who'd love to empty their closets of outgrown and barely used Halloween outfits. Thrift stores are another great option for finding or putting together a unique costume.

Your children may say they want to be the exact same store-bought princess or superhero as every other kid, but they might be swayed with a few inspirational images online (a.k.a. Pinterest). How about a bat outfit from an old black umbrella? Two large cardboard boxes turn the twins into a pair of dice. This option invites creative thinking from the whole family and often results in contest-winning outfits.

Those cheap packages of Halloween makeup can be pretty scary in terms of their content, which includes petroleum and heavy metals. Check the Environmental Working Group's Skin Deep Cosmetics Safety Database for non-toxic options. Or use natural items from your kitchen to create your own makeup including wounds, warts and fake blood.

GREEN YOUR Halloween

25% of all the candy sold yearly in the U.S. is purchased for Halloween. Reduce both sugar and packaging with alternative treats like tattoos, bubbles, shells, gems, loose change or dried fruit.

Ancient celts carved pumpkins to scare evil spirits and to carry embers from their sacred bonfire. Grow your own! Pumpkins offer natural decoration, fun activities and nutritional snacks high in **VITAMINS A, B, IRON, POTASSIUM AND PROTEIN.**

The **2ND SATURDAY** in October is National Costume Swap Day, an eco-friendly way to wear a new costume every year.

Studies found **100%** of Halloween makeup to contain **TOXIC HEAVY METALS** including cadmium, arsenic, mercury and lead. Did you know you can create your own edible makeup from food?

1966 The year *It's the Great Pumpkin, Charlie Brown* debuted in which pillow-cases find a second life as earth-friendly ghost costumes and treat bags.

Design: DonnaDeForbesCreates.com | Sources: HealthyStuff.org, History.com

ACTIVITIES

- This is the perfect season for heading out to the country. Many farms operate fall festivals, corn mazes, hay rides, apple picking, haunted houses and, of course, pumpkin patches.

- Host a pumpkin carving party. Smaller gourds can be carved too. Save the seeds; bake and eat them lightly salted. Afterwards, compost the pumpkin or donate it to your town's zoo for the animals.

- Hate the mess of pumpkins? With a little orange paint and some repurposed round containers, you can create your own solar-powered, eco Jack-o-Lanterns. Search online for "recycled Halloween crafts" and you'll get lots of DIY tutorials that turn regular household items into holiday treasures.

- Watch *It's the Great Pumpkin, Charlie Brown*. It's a family classic with some eco references... like using pillowcases as trick-or-treat bags.

- Enjoy the fall weather with outdoor fun such as costume parades, family bike rides or games of graveyard hide-n-seek.

- While trick-or-treating is the main activity for kids, there are alternatives to receiving boatloads of sugary candy. Options including sending excess candy to U.S. troops overseas or participating in the Candy Buy-Back Program where dentists offer kids cash or coupons for their candy.

FOOD AND DRINK

- Stand out from the pack by giving out candy that makes a difference. Dark chocolate (with at least 70% cacao) is full of healthy antioxidants. Fair Trade chocolate means the farmers who grow the cocoa are treated well. Kids always remember the house that gives out the "big candy bar." In my day it was usually Hershey's, but I love Endangered Species chocolate bars—they come in different varieties and give a percentage of profits to wildlife organizations. Visit GreenHalloween.org for a detailed list of companies that sell certified-organic chocolate and other candy.

- If your neighborhood is a small one where everybody knows each other, homemade treats are an option. Make them nut-free to avoid allergy problems. Or pass out organic apples.

- When possible, buy treats in bulk to minimize the amount of packaging waste.

- Grow your own pumpkins. They require a lot of space but look pretty and are fairly easy to maintain. Plan accordingly—northern locations should plant pumpkins by late May; southern locations by early July.

- Autumn calls for baking. Spend a family afternoon making seasonal foods from apple pies to apple cider, pumpkin bread to pumpkin soup.

Out-of-the-Box Celebration Ideas

While the essence of Halloween is death and the supernatural, it doesn't need to be scary. Incorporate these themes in positive ways.

- Kids do think about death, so rather than avoid the topic, encourage them to share their thoughts and questions. Talk openly about fears, and clear up any misconceptions. Explaining death as a transition to something else (rather than "the end") may make it less scary. Honor your own deceased relatives by visiting their gravesites, looking through photo albums or sharing stories and memories about them.

- Use Halloween to explore stories of the supernatural or biographies of famous dead people. Start reading the Harry Potter book series, which deals with ghosts, death and all things magical. My mother makes it a ritual to read the entire series and watch the films every year.

- Camping isn't just for summer. Crisp fall nights make it more fun to cozy up in a sleeping bag and gather around the campfire. Being outside at night has a magical feel about it just perfect for this holiday. You could make a tradition of Halloween camping, even if it's just in your own backyard. What better way to share ghost stories?

- Elicit one of the original essences of Samhain—focus on the season's harvest by putting your garden to bed for winter. Then hold a harvest feast with contributions from friends and family.

Chapter 7:
Thanksgiving

History *and* Meaning

Now a day of family, food and football, Thanksgiving was initially a harvest celebration of the Pilgrims in the New World.

Although they weren't known as Pilgrims then—that name stuck when orator Daniel Webster referred to them as "Pilgrim Fathers" during a bicentennial celebration. In 1607, they were just a radical Puritan group who broke from the Church of England, escaped to the Netherlands for a while, then set sail for America. The religious separatists traveled aboard the *Mayflower* and landed off the coast of Massachusetts in 1620.

A harsh winter and contagious disease killed half of the original 102 passengers. Come spring, those who remained settled ashore in Plymouth and were befriended by Squanto, a Native American from the Pawtuxet tribe. Squanto helped the Pilgrims survive by teaching them how to sow corn, catch fish and extract sap from maple trees. He also introduced them to the local Wampanoag tribe with whom the colonists maintained a harmonious relationship for fifty years.

The Thanksgiving Menu

Thanks to Squanto's help, the Pilgrims saw a successful corn harvest in 1621 and celebrated that with a three-day feast— now known as the "first Thanksgiving." Attended by 53 colonists and 90 Wampanoag, the menu likely consisted of many fowl (turkey, swan, duck and goose), deer, lobster, shellfish, stuffing (herbs, onions and oats), corn and pumpkin.

Although native to the area, cranberries were not mentioned in historical accounts of the first meal; potatoes had not yet made their way to New England; and a lack of refrigeration, butter or expensive sugar made pies impossible.

Today, thanksgiving feasts vary according to region. While turkey, cranberries and pumpkin remain traditional New England food, people incorporate crab and sauerkraut in Maryland, chiles in New Mexico, persimmon puddings in Indiana and sweet potatoes in the South.

The Name "Thanksgiving"

Giving thanks for a successful harvest was an ancient tradition among many cultures that often revolved around feasting and recreation. The ancient Romans celebrated Cerelia in October with music, parades, sports and homage to Ceres, the goddess of corn. Solemn days of thanksgiving and prayer occurred regularly among the Puritans of New England. Native Americans such as the Wampanoag regularly offered thanks to the Creator for their food.

The Pilgrims' Thanksgiving of 1621 was certainly not the first harvest feast in America, but perhaps due to its records and its good story, it is recognized as the birth of the American Thanksgiving.

The first national Thanksgiving was proclaimed by the Continental Congress in 1777 as a solemn event. President Lincoln is often credited with declaring it a national holiday in 1863, however Thanksgiving did not become a fixed annual event until 1941 when Congress permanently marked it as the fourth Thursday in November.

DID YOU KNOW?

- Franklin Roosevelt tried to change the date in 1939. He made Thanksgiving one week earlier to appease merchants who wanted an even longer shopping season, but the plan backfired.

- The first TV dinner was Thanksgiving leftovers—created by Swanson in 1953 as a way to use the excess turkey they had bought that year.

- Legend says the turkey was named by Christopher Columbus who, thinking he was in India, used the Indian word for peacock: *tuka*.

- Native Americans used cranberries as a food, a fabric dye and a medicine to treat arrow wounds.

Modern Thanksgiving Traditions

The New York City Thanksgiving *Parade* first hit the streets in 1924. It was initiated by Macy's department store employees, many who were immigrants wanting to celebrate their new American heritage with a European-style festival. The parade —with floats, bands, costumes, live animals and Santa Claus— became a huge and continuing success.

Football and Thanksgiving have been a combination on the collegiate level since 1876. By the end of the century, thousands of college and high school football games took place on Thanksgiving Day, including championship match-ups like Princeton vs. Yale. The National Football League joined in the Thanksgiving tradition in 1934 when the newly relocated Detroit Lions played the World Champion Chicago Bears as a way to attract more fans.

As far back as the 19th century, people viewed Thanksgiving as the kickoff to the holiday *shopping* season, and department stores took advantage of this by offering big sales.

While the term "Black Friday" was first associated with a stock market panic in 1864, it gained new life in the 1960s when a Philadelphia newspaper used the phrase to describe the day-after-Thanksgiving store crowds. By the 1990s, Black Friday had become a shopper's dream of extended hours and door-buster deals, and it is typically the biggest shopping day of the season.

A Day of Gratitude

At its heart, Thanksgiving is a day of enjoying food and family. In the United States, it still ranks as the busiest travel time of the year as folks journey miles to spend time with loved ones.

Although Thanksgiving is considered an American holiday, fall harvest feasts are celebrated around the world under different names and at different times, depending on the country's growing season. Canada celebrates Thanksgiving with parades and turkey in October. Korea's Chu-Sok is a three-day festival honoring family and food. Their traditional dish is Songpyon, a mix of rice, beans, sesame seeds and chestnuts. One of India's harvest festivals is Pongal, celebrated in January with bonfires and feasting.

Simple Tips for Greening Thanksgiving

DECORATION

- Use non-toxic cleaners for your pre-holiday house cleaning. You'll find that many products from your kitchen can double as household cleaners, saving you money and eliminating nasty chemical odors. The best cleaners don't use much more than vinegar, baking soda and essential oils for a disinfecting and pleasant smelling clean.

- Set the table with natural fabrics, reusable dinnerware and dripless beeswax candles. Cloth napkins can be made from scraps of fabric, old sheets or clothing and can even be personalized for family members.

- Instead of buying plastic centerpieces, make a cornucopia of nuts, apples and colorful gourds in a natural wicker basket or a seasonal decoration of leaves, pinecones, acorns and dried herbs. Kids can make place cards from recycled construction paper or try something unique like writing guests' name on collected shells and rocks.

ACTIVITIES

- Elicit the holiday's essence of giving thanks. Go around the table and share something you're grateful for besides the abundant feast before you. The past few years, my mother has had everyone write their thoughts of thanks directly onto the white tablecloth. Each year, she brings it out again and we get to reread previous years' memories—including those of passed grandparents—before adding a new one.

- Watching televised football is a Thanksgiving ritual in many American homes. However, couchsitting is not the best way to digest such a huge meal, and it can often bring out the grumpies in little kids. Trade in an hour of television for playing football or some other sport in the backyard. It's interactive, connecting and a great way to work off some of that dinner. Alternatively, attend a local school football game.

  Not a fan of football? Go for a neighborhood walk and listen to the leaves crunch. Take the kids to the playground. Doing something outdoors, even for a short time, invigorates your body as well as the energy of the group.

- Board games are great holiday fun. In a large gathering, you can have several games going at once, and then rotate groups. Make it part of the holiday tradition by introducing a different game every year. (This doesn't mean you have to buy it new. I've found many a complete game at yard sales and thrift shops.) You can add a green theme if you like with games like Earthopoly or cooperative board games where players work together instead of against one another.

- Are there several family and friends who live near each other? Make a progressive party of Thanksgiving instead of leaving one person with the bulk of the work. A progressive party means guests gather at one house for the first course and walk from house to house for other courses (and activities) throughout the evening. For example, the first house might offer appetizers and an icebreaker game. Move on to house #2 for the main course. Then take a long, digestion-aiding walk to house #3 for dessert and live music.

- **Travel Tips** Thanksgiving is the most traveled weekend of the year. If you're leaving town, consider buying carbon offsets, which are a way of alleviating guilt and supporting carbon-reducing projects like wind farms. Find out more at sites like CarbonFund.org or TerraPass.com.

  Choose the train or bus before a car or airplane. They create fewer carbon emissions per passenger, and they'll keep you away from crowds and long lines (only about 2-3% of Americans travel by bus or train over Thanksgiving). If you do fly, consider the greenness of an airline. Does it support sustainable food options, recycling or fuel-conservation programs? A little online research can tell you which airlines are currently ranked as the most eco-friendly.

FOOD AND DRINK

- **Talkin' Turkey** I love my Thanksgiving turkey, so I was upset when I learned that the Broad-Breasted White Butterball turkey we're used to was developed in the 1960s by factory farms with the goal of creating the most white meat in the shortest amount of time. This means those turkeys can't walk, fly, procreate and are susceptible to disease. They're raised in cramped quarters, force fed corn mush fortified with large doses of antibiotics and later injected with vegetable oils to add "flavor." Yum.

  If this is not your idea of a good meal, there are other turkey breeds besides the Butterball. Seek out "heritage breeds" from places like Heritage Food USA or The American Livestock Breed Conservancy. Heritage turkeys breed naturally and live a drug-free outdoor life.

  You might want to know how to decipher those turkey labels. Here's a general guide. (The Humane Society has a more detailed list of labels.) "Organic" turkeys are fed grains grown without pesticides; "Vegetarian-fed" birds

TIPS FOR A GREENER Thanksgiving

| DECOR | ACTIVITIES | HISTORY | FOOD |

DECOR

Plastics represent

12.7%

(or 32 million tons) of total **household waste yearly.** They leach chemicals into our bodies, groundwater and wildlife. Green your decorations (and protect your health) by using natural wicker baskets, fabric tablecloths and centerpieces derived from nature: gourds, nuts, pinecones, fruits and colorful leaves.

ACTIVITIES

Thanksgiving and football have been a tradition since 1876. Trade in some time watching the game for playing one outside. Just **2.5 hours** of activity can burn off **1300 calories** of your holiday meal.

42,000,000

Americans travel by car or airplane over the long weekend. Avoid crowds and reduce fuel emissions by taking the train or bus.

HISTORY

1941
The year Congress made Thanksgiving a fixed annual holiday on the 4th Thursday in November.

47%
of Americans **shop on Black Friday.** 23% even camp outside stores the night before. **Buy Nothing Day** emerged in the 1990s as an anti-consumerist response now observed in many countries.

FOOD

46 million

turkeys are killed for the holiday even though the bird was not the main dish of the first Thanksgiving. Green your meal by cooking more local foods like the Pilgrims did; they also feasted on corn, lobster, deer, pumpkin and swan.

Composting vegetables, fruit, eggs and coffee grinds helps reduce the **36 million tons** of food waste sent to landfills yearly.

Design: DonnaDeForbesCreates.com
Sources: History.com, epa.gov, AAA.com, active.com, ScientificAmerican.com.

receive no meat, but this means they're not allowed outside where they can peck for bugs; "Cage-free" turkeys won't be kept in cages but it doesn't guarantee that they have access to the outdoors; "Free range" birds are not fed hormones or confined, but their "range" may be in a barn or on a concrete floor. "Pastured" turkeys roam around on pasture eating grass and insects, so they may not be considered organic.

With so many labels potentially driving you crazy, your best bet is to seek out a local farmer who can tell you all you want to know about your turkey. Visit LocalHarvest. org to find a turkey farm near you.

Animal lovers who cringe at the idea of 46 million turkeys being killed for Thanksgiving may want to adopt a turkey for the holiday instead. Or dine on the vegetarian alternative, Tofurky.

- Green your Thanksgiving meal by going local like the Pilgrims did. Their menu wasn't centered around turkey (and they had no potatoes), so don't feel you're bucking tradition by choosing foods native to your region. Remember, turkey was a rather random pick for the traditional Thanksgiving meal. It could just as easily have been lobster or venison.

- Consider the dietary needs of your guests. You'll find plenty of vegetarian and vegan Thanksgiving recipes online. And there's nothing wrong with making Thanksgiving a potluck (we do). It takes the pressure off, and guests enjoy contributing to the holiday meal.

- Keep food waste to a minimum. Do you really need four different pies? Traditionally, a main dish, four sides and one dessert is a good rule of thumb for the Thanksgiving meal. Have a plan for leftover food. If you can't stomach turkey leftovers for the next five days, be sure to send some home with guests. Store leftovers in BPA-free reusable containers rather than using Saran wrap or aluminum foil.

- Compost leftover vegetable and fruit scraps. Egg shells, coffee grinds and tea leaves can be composted too.

- Be energy-efficient by cooking multiple dishes in the oven at the same time. On the stovetop, use the smallest pot necessary for cooking an item, and cover it to reduce evaporation.
- Look into organic wine and beer. Or serve a traditional wassail.

Out-of-the-Box Celebration Ideas

The essence of Thanksgiving is gratitude—appreciating the season's abundance and sharing it with others.

- One of the best ways to appreciate what you have is to be around those who have less. Volunteer as a family at a soup kitchen or other local organization serving food to people in need.

- The Pilgrims stepped outside their comfort zone to get to know their Native American neighbors. Use this season to snap out of your own rut. Introduce yourself to neighbors you've never met, that family you always see at church or the couple waiting in the airport next to you. Who knows what potential relationships might spark?

- If you don't live near family, make your own. My husband and I live in another state and don't always go home for the holiday. Many years we have hosted an "orphans" Thanksgiving consisting of friends who don't have family nearby, including our good friends from India who now look forward to turkey and mashed potatoes every November.

- Why not commemorate the holiday where it first began? Take a family trip to Plimouth Plantation in Massachusetts for an annual Harvest or Thanksgiving Dinner with the Pilgrims. Enjoy traditional dishes, English tales and song, and lively role-playing. During your trip, you can tour a bit of American history by stepping aboard *Mayflower II*, a full-scale reproduction of the original, or meeting Native People at the Wampanoag Homesite. Plan early, as the Thanksgiving Dinner fills up quickly.

- Opt out of Black Friday and honor its alternative, Buy Nothing Day, which is sort of like a detox from consumerism. Instead, celebrate the Friday after Thanksgiving with a hike in nature, family movie time or coming up with handmade gift ideas for Christmas. The Tuesday after Thanksgiving is gaining clout as #GivingTuesday—you might want to focus on this national day of charitable giving to kickoff the holiday season.

TOP 5 STATS ABOUT BLACK FRIDAY

- Around 47% of Americans shop on Black Friday.
- New York City residents spend the most money (about $259 each).
- Consumer spending in 2012 surpassed $59 billion.
- About 23% of shoppers camp out at a store on Thanksgiving night.
- Top retailers include Walmart, Best Buy, Target and Apple.

Chapter 8:
Christmas and Winter Holidays

History and Meaning

Centuries before the birth of Jesus, mid-winter was a time of celebration around the world. Wary of the shortening days and loss of sunlight, ancient cultures gathered together to pray for the return of the sun. Their celebrations centered around fire and light and marked the Winter Solstice—the shortest day of the year—usually around December 21.

With the end of the agricultural season, mid-winter was a natural time for feasting before the darkest, coldest days of the year.

People of northern Europe (including England and Scandinavia) celebrated Yule on December 21 with a large log they would set on fire to "wake up the sun." People sang and feasted until the Yule log burned out, usually about 12 days later. In Europe, cattle were often slaughtered in December so cows would not have to be fed during the winter season. This surplus of fresh meat was another cause for celebration.

Farther south, the Romans celebrated Saturnalia in honor of Saturn, the god of agriculture. For several hedonistic weeks, the Romans ate, drank and turned the social order upside down: slaves became masters, peasants ruled the city and business and schools shut down. December 25 marked the rebirth of the Unconquered Sun, or the return of longer days after the Winter Solstice.

The birth of Jesus was not even commemorated by the Catholic Church until the 4th century when Pope Julius I chose December 25 to mark the occasion. Since Jesus' actual birthday was likely in the spring, common belief is that the Church chose the date to capitalize on a time of year when public celebrations were already popular. By the Middle Ages, the celebration of Christmas had almost completely replaced the original pagan festivities.

Back then Christmas was celebrated by attending church and then partying in a carnival-like atmosphere. Upper classes entertained less fortunate ones; the poor begged for food and drink at the houses of the rich; and a "Lord of Misrule" was crowned. In post-Reformation England and Puritan America, such a rowdy Christmas holiday was frowned upon and even banned in some areas.

Our modern version of Christmas—a family-centered day of peace and nostalgia—was actually invented in the 19th-century Victorian era. It's transformation from raucous celebration was inspired largely by several popular stories: Washington Irving's *The Sketchbook of Geoffrey Crayon, gent.* and Charles Dickens' *A Christmas Carol.*

During this period of widespread class conflict in America, the message of peace, charity and goodwill toward all in both Irving's and Dickens' stories was very appealing. With attitudes toward the needs of children also beginning to change, Christmas seemed the perfect holiday to spread cheer and lavish children with gifts.

Americans unearthed old customs from the church and borrowed new ones from immigrants to fashion the holiday into a cornucopia of traditions from across the centuries. This new family-centric Christmas blossomed over the next several decades until, in 1870, it was declared a U.S. federal holiday.

DID YOU KNOW?

- Christmas was cancelled in 1645 when Oliver Cromwell and his Puritan followers took over England.

- 98% of all Christmas trees are grown on farms with 77 million planted every year. Each one takes about 6-8 years to mature.

- The U.S. postal service delivers about 15.8 billion cards, letters and packages between Thanksgiving and Christmas Eve.

- The Hanukkah dreidel was originally used as a decoy by Jews illegally studying the Torah. When Greek soldiers came by, students quickly switched books for the dreidel gambling game.

Where did Santa Claus come from?

The story of Santa Claus has its roots in a monk named St. Nicholas from the 3rd century A.D. The legends surrounding this popular saint speak of his generosity and kindness toward children. St. Nicholas first appeared in America in 1773 when Dutch families gathered to honor the December anniversary of his death. Translated in Dutch as *Sint Nikolass* (with the nickname *Sinter Klaas*), Nicholas became the patron saint of New York and was popularized in stories by Washington Irving.

It was Clement Clarke Moore's 1822 poem "An Account of a Visit from St. Nicholas" that inspired our modern vision of a high-flying, portly Santa Claus with a sleigh of reindeer. In 1881, political cartoonist Thomas Nast added to the myth with his drawings of Santa sporting a white beard and fur-trimmed red suit, accompanied by elves and Mrs. Claus.

Across the ocean, St. Nicholas inspired gift-giving figures in other cultures as well: Christkind or Kris Kringle in Germany and Switzerland; Father Christmas in England; Pere Noel in France and Babouschka in Russia.

The Christmas Tree

Evergreen trees have been popular in winter festivals since ancient times, from the Norse to the Celts to the Romans. Some believed evergreens kept evil spirits away. Others decorated their homes with boughs of pine, spruce and fir as a reminder that things would indeed grow again come spring.

The evergreen as a Christmas icon is credited to 16th century Germans who brought them into their homes for decoration. Immigrants brought the Christmas tree, or *Tannenbaum* to Pennsylvania, although the custom did not catch on until 1846 following a publicized sketch of Queen Victoria's family posing around a Christmas tree. Imitating the popular Queen made the Christmas tree a tradition in England, the United States and Canada.

Early decorations included homemade ornaments and food (nuts, apples and popcorn). To Christians, a candle on top of the tree symbolized the birth of Christ as the Light of the World. The invention of electricity led to glowing lights for the tree, and it wasn't long before every American household had to have one.

The tradition of New York's Rockefeller Center Christmas tree began in 1931 with a small, unadorned one. Today, it exhibits more than 25,000 lights.

Other Symbols

German settlers in America brought with them gingerbread houses, cookies and Advent calendars. England gave us Christmas card greetings (in 1830) and caroling, as musicians wandered from town to town singing for money. The Celts hung mistletoe for good luck; sneaking a kiss beneath it became common during the restrained Victorian era. Putting out stockings (or shoes) to receive gifts was a Dutch tradition associated with St. Nicholas.

A Day of Joy

Although Christmas has evolved over centuries from pagan sun celebrations to religious feasts of Jesus to family connection, the heart of the holiday has been about joyous celebration. Today, some form of Christmas is honored in nearly every country, making it the most celebrated holiday in the world.

Winter Holidays Around the World

Hanukkah This Jewish Festival of Lights falls in November or December and commemorates the Maccabean Revolt and the rededication of the Second Temple in Jerusalem. Their menorah candelabrum, which only had enough olive oil to burn for a single day, continued to burn for eight nights. Jews honor this miracle with an eight-night Hanukkah celebration that centers around lighting the menorah, feasting and exchanging gifts.

The Green Menorah is a modern-day movement in the Jewish community to renew the miracle of Hanukkah and reduce oil consumption—to use one day's oil to meet eight days' needs—so that U.S. oil consumption is reduced by seven-eighths by the year 2020.

Diwali is the Hindu Festival of Lights celebrated in parts of India and Britain every October or November. Although the legends vary, Diwali is largely a celebration of light over darkness and is marked by feasts, exchanging gifts, cleaning the home and massive fireworks displays. Children make lanterns called *deepas* that light up the streets for five days.

In Mexico, a Christmas tradition of **Las Posadas** mimics the travels of Jesus' parents, Joseph and Mary, seeking shelter in Bethlehem. For eight nights people parade from house to house; neighbors invite each other in and celebrate with food and candles.

Scandinavian countries celebrate **St. Lucia Day** on December 13. Towns elect a St. Lucia who leads a procession of young girls and boys dressed in white and bearing candles. The festival ushers in the Christmas season and symbolizes hope and light for the coming winter.

Kwanzaa is a modern holiday based on an ancient African harvest celebration. Beginning December 26, family and friends gather to share gifts, food, music and stories. A candle on the *kinara* is lit each of the seven days until January 1. Kwanzaa honors seven ideas of community and family, and the holiday often involves games, crafts and paying respect to ancestors.

Simple Tips for Greening Christmas and Winter Holidays

With 25% more trash created during the winter holidays, it's an excellent time to go green. There are lots of ways you can make some eco-friendly changes without sacrificing holiday cheer. Even one or two actions are enough to make a difference, and who knows? It might even grease the wheels for future change.

DECORATION

- **_Trees and Trimming_** Should you get a real or artificial tree? That is often the big eco question. Generally speaking, a live tree is the greener and less toxic option. Most people don't keep a fake tree long enough to make a difference, and Christmas tree farms offer many benefits to the earth, including increased oxygen, soil stability and animal habitat. Plus, after the holidays, a real tree can be turned into compost or mulch. Most communities offer curbside pickup or a central drop-off location for this purpose.

  Regarding tree ornaments, you have several options. Using what you already have is an ideal scenario, which may include ornaments you made from popsicle sticks in grade school. In our house, it is these handmade family ornaments that elicit the most excitement, especially from my daughter who has a fondness for her grandmother's painted ceramic sun and the yarn-spun "Mariachi" Santa.

  If buying new, choose ornaments made from natural materials like wood, wool, silk, natural rubber or anything made from recycled components. Buying locally from holiday bazaars and craft fairs supports your local artisans and avoids fuel emissions from shipping.

CHRISTMAS
TIPS FOR A GREENER HOLIDAY

BUY A REAL TREE. 77 million Christmas trees are planted by farms each year; they increase oxygen, soil stability and animal habitat. Many communities will pick up your tree curbside for mulching after the holiday.

DECORATE WITH LED LIGHTS. These bulbs use up to 90% less energy than incandescents and don't release mercury as CFLs do when broken. Plus, you shouldn't have to replace an LED bulb for **20 YEARS.**

DO LESS. Buy one less present, attend one less event, take one less shopping trip. You'll save resources and your sanity.

Americans throw out **25%** more trash over the winter holidays. **BE LESS DISPOSABLE** by sending e-cards, wrapping with recycled papers and choosing more sustainable gifts (locally made, natural materials, less packaging).

Americans spend about **$6 billion** on holiday decorations. Change up your decor by hosting a swap with family and friends.

MAKE KINDNESS YOUR GIFT as did the original Santa Claus, a monk named St. Nicholas who spread joy by helping others.

Design: DonnaDeForbesCreates.com | Sources: History.com, EPA.gov, mnn.com, NRF.com

You can always mimic ancient tradition by decorating the tree with edibles: nuts, apples, cranberries and popcorn. Then when you take the tree down, you can eat the ornaments or toss them outside for the squirrels to feast on.

- *The Lowdown on Lighting* When it comes to lighting, LEDs (light-emitting diode) are the most energy-efficient bulbs, even more so than the widely-known CFLs (compact fluorescent light bulbs). LEDs come in warm and cool white as well as holiday colors. While LED lights do carry a heftier price tag, you shouldn't have to change a bulb for 20 years, so it's worth it. LEDs are cool to the touch and use half as much energy as CFLs (and up to 90% less than incandescents).

  Speaking of which, if you still have incandescent lights lurking around your house, it's time to make the switch. Incandescents contribute to so much greenhouse gases that some countries have banned them, and the U.S. has been phasing them out.

  Outside, you can decorate with solar-powered lights, which require just a few hours of sunlight to charge and have the extra benefit of not requiring an electrical outlet.

  Did you know you can recycle your old or broken Christmas lights? Call your local Home Depot or Walmart, as they often run programs during the holidays. Or visit HolidayLEDs.com. From October through February you can mail them your old lights and receive a coupon for new LEDs.

- Sometimes nothing sets a holiday mood faster than a glowing fireplace. Gas and pellet stoves burn cleaner and are more energy efficient than the traditional stone hearth. As for the logs, there are many green options out there. Search online for "eco fire logs" and you'll find brands made from recycled cardboard, mill waste or even coffee grounds.

Compared to wood, these fire logs tend to emit less carbon dioxide and create less creosote in your chimney.

- Less is more when it comes to decoration. Think twice before buying this year's faddish, disposable holiday item. Choose décor made from eco-friendly materials that will last. Pack them away carefully so that bringing out the familiar holiday decorations every year becomes a tradition in itself. My sisters and I loved unwrapping the ceramic Nativity set painted by my mother and fought to set up the wooden tabletop Christmas tree, even with its missing pieces.

- Using fresh greenery to decorate the house is a great way to bring the outdoors in. Make wreaths and mantel boughs from tree trimmings for a natural pine scent. If you still have plastic garland from previous years, it's better to get as much use from it as possible rather than to toss it into the nearest landfill.

- Consider what decorations your family can make instead of buy. Can old Christmas cards become holiday place mats? What about outgrown rain boots as "stockings" to fill? We made a simple Advent calendar from an old holiday gift box. The Internet is filled with oodles of DIY holiday-inspired crafts, many made by upcycling materials.

- When you're done with your holiday decorations, post them on Craigslist or Freecycle before throwing them out. Or find out how you can donate them to a family in need.

ACTIVITIES

- Host a holiday decoration swap. People tire of their décor after years of use, but rather than send it off to the landfill, try trading it first. Your reindeer lawn ornament might be just what your neighbor has been wanting, while you love his snowman window display. This would be a great activity in lieu of shopping on Thanksgiving weekend.

- Keep party waste to a minimum. Light the space with holiday LEDs and beeswax candles. Serve food on reusable or biodegradable tableware and linens. Offer homemade drinks in pitchers rather than purchasing individual, store-bought bottles.

- Growing up, my family would drive around neighborhoods seeking out fabulous light displays. While enjoyable, it also wasted a lot of fuel. Opt instead for attending your town's tree lighting ceremony. Or exchange the driving for neighborhood caroling.

- Make your own tree ornaments. Seek out objects from nature such as pinecones or shells, which the kids can decorate. Fold recycled paper into origami. Hold a contest to see who can make the most unique ornament using repurposed household items (buttons, jewelry, scrap wood, hardware, broken toys...).

- Bake an eco-friendly gingerbread house. Think beyond the traditional ingredients: use cage-free eggs, Fair Trade molasses and non-candy items like almonds, dates or sunflower seeds. Does your house have chocolate bar solar panels? A wind turbine made of dried peppers? An egg shell for a rain barrel?

- Make your own holiday tradition or game. When my daughter was four, we began a hide-n-seek game using the Santa Claus ornament my mother sewed in the 1970s. (He somehow became dubbed "Mariachi" Santa by my husband.) Throughout the season, we take turns hiding him in the house. Santa has been discovered in cereal boxes, underneath shelves, inside shoes and, once, my daughter hid him so well that nobody found Santa until spring.

- Around the winter holidays, sometimes the greenest thing you can do is to *do less*. Buy one less gift, take one less shopping trip, attend one less event. Regain some much-needed calm and time.

GIFTS

Give some thought before tossing items into your shopping cart. Christmas doesn't need to be a time of giving and receiving more unwanted stuff. Reach beyond obligation to consider what your friends and family really need. Often people prefer the intangibles—time, an experience or a service—over things.

- About 1.6 billion Christmas cards are purchased every year. You can reduce the amount of paper with electronic, recycled or plantable seeded cards and gift tags. Create your own personalized video message. Turn greetings cards you've received in previous years into postcards by tearing off the cover. I've always enjoyed receiving those annual family newsletters that provide updates and photos from rarely-seen friends. We went electronic with ours a few years back, and it saves me both time (addressing cards) and money (stamps).

- Make a commitment to purchasing eco-friendly gifts this year. Seek out handmade crafts or products made sustainably. Support local merchants instead of big box stores. Buy Fair Trade gifts, which usually cut out the middleman to provide artisans and their communities with decent profits. Look for the Fair Trade Federation logo.

- Gift cards may seem like the easy way out, but they are a fairly green option. Gift cards require no packaging, minimal wrapping and can be reloaded or recycled afterwards.

- What do you get for the person who has it all? Consider gifts that give back: purchase carbon offsets, adopt an endangered species, plant a tree in someone's name or buy from a company that regularly donates a percentage of its profits to charities.

Make charitable donations in someone's name to a nonprofit that makes you think of them, such as Arbor Day Foundation for the nature lover or Good Sports for the sports fan (they provide sports equipment to disadvantaged youth). Get inspired at CharityNavigator.org and JustGive. org.

TOP 5 WEBSITES FOR ECO-FRIENDLY TOYS

- GreenToys.com
- PlanToys.com
- NovaNatural.com
- HolgateToy.com
- Palumba.com

- Put your heart and talent into a homemade gift: a book of photos or special memories; an original poem or story; a hand-carved toy.

- Less can be more. Rather than stockpiling a humongous pile of presents for the kids, do something creative with fewer gifts like a holiday treasure hunt. Hide presents throughout the house with written clues the kids need to solve. It's surprisingly fun and makes the gift opening experience last longer.

- Go green with your gift wrapping by choosing 100% recycled or Fair Trade gift wrap, reusing gift bags you've received or getting creative with any number of materials:

newspaper, your child's artwork, magazine pages, bubble wrap, burlap bags, fabric scraps, etc. If you go with the treasure hunt idea above, you don't even have to wrap the gifts.

When mailing packages, protect gifts with crumpled newspaper, fabric or by reusing air-filled bags or biodegradable peanut packing.

Out-of-the-Box Celebration Ideas

The essence of Christmas, Hanukkah and the Winter Solstice is joy—celebrating light in the world.

- Spread the idea of giving beyond your own circle. Use this time of year to volunteer at a soup kitchen, read to seniors at a nursing home or donate to an organization that helps those less fortunate. Since Sofie was born, we make an annual donation to Heifer.org, and she takes much joy in choosing that year's animal. It's one of the few ways to teach our kids that Christmas is as much about giving as it is getting.

- Power down for the Winter Solstice. At this time of year when people seem compelled to buy more and do more, it's often a relief to get off the holiday rat race and introduce peace and stillness. It reminds us that the holidays are about regaining a certain joy and balance that cannot be found in presents or parties. It connects us with our ancestors whose lives depended on the sun and reminds us of all that we take for granted.

My family "powers down" by unplugging our clocks, lights and electronics to connect with nature and with each other without distraction. (We do use the heat and the stove.) When the sun goes down, we light our home with candles and go to bed earlier than usual. Past Winter Solstices have included candlelit drum circles, nature walks and studying cloud formations from the bed of a pickup truck.

- Skip town and experience the winter holidays in another country. Exposing your family to other cultural celebrations may inject some much-needed energy and inspire ideas for your future holidays.

- Whether you're Jewish or not, you can honor the Green Menorah movement by making eight green changes over eight days. Assign an area of your life to each day (home, food, transportation, clothing, office, etc.) and commit to some small action.

- Trade in parties and shopping for quiet ways to honor the season. Make a nightly ritual of lighting a candle, reading an inspirational piece and sharing favorite holiday memories or hopes for the future. Read Washington Irving's and Charles Dickens' stories that inspired the modern American Christmas. Create family wish lists of places to visit, activities to enjoy and dreams to pursue.

- Be the light in the world for someone else. Use the kids' winter break to try a volunteer vacation that might involve building houses in Costa Rica or doing trail maintenance for U.S. national parks. Such a trip will shift your perspective about the things that are really important.

More *to* Celebrate

On my Eco-Mothering blog, I wrote posts about unique, lesser-known and gently green holidays to celebrate throughout the year. Almost every day of the year has one or several causes assigned to it.

I've included here a handful of the more earth-friendly ones to show you that greening your holidays can go beyond the major ones. Because the actual dates often change from year to year (e.g.: the first Saturday of March), I've only included the name of the holidays within each month. Look online for actual dates by year.

Pick whichever holidays appeal to you and get out there and celebrate!

JANUARY

Cut Your Energy Costs Day
National Bird Day
National Blood Donor Month
National Seed Swap Day
Penguin Awareness Day

FEBRUARY

Bird-Feeding Month
Polar Bear Day
World Day of Social Justice
World Wetlands Day
World Whale Day

MARCH

Biodiesel Day
Day of Unplugging
Manatee Appreciation Day
Plant a Flower Day
Spring Equinox
World Water Day

APRIL

Arbor Day
Dolphin Day
Earth Day
Microvolunteering Day
Walk to Work Day
World Health Day

MAY

Endangered Species Day
International Day of Families
Learn About Composting Day
National Bike Month
World Fair Trade Day

JUNE

Great Outdoors Month
Summer Solstice
World Blood Donor Day
World Environment Day
World Oceans Day

JULY

Independence From Meat Day
International Plastic Bag Free Day
International Tiger Day
Shark Awareness Day
World Population Day

AUGUST

Garage Sale Day
National Honeybee Day
Water Quality Month
Women's Equality Day
World Breastfeeding Week
World Elephant Day
World Humanitarian Day

SEPTEMBER

Coastal Cleanup Day
Fall Equinox
International Day of Charity
International Day of Peace
World Car Free Day

OCTOBER

International Day of Nonviolence
Make a Difference Day
World Animal Day
World Habitat Day
World Vegetarian Day

NOVEMBER

America Recycles Day
Buy Nothing Day
Giving Tuesday
National Adoption Day
Take a Hike Day

DECEMBER

Human Rights Month
International Mountain Day
International Volunteer Day
Regifting Day
Winter Solstice
World Wildlife Conservation Day

Resources for You

FOOD AND DRINK

Sourcing Local Food and Farms / Sustainable Restaurants:
http://www.localharvest.org
http://www.eatwellguide.org
https://www.dinegreen.com

Fair Trade, GMO-free and Organic Candy:
https://www.naturalcandystore.com

Deciphering Meat and Dairy Labels:
http://www.humanesociety.org/issues/confinement_farm/facts/
meat_dairy_labels.html

Deciphering Egg Labels:
http://www.humanesociety.org/issues/confinement_farm/facts/
guide_egg_labels.html

Adopt a Turkey for Thanksgiving
http://www.farmsanctuary.org/giving/adopt-a-turkey/

Organic Beer:
http://www.dummies.com/how-to/content/choosing-an-organic-
beer.html

Organic Wines:
http://organicwinefind.com

Biodynamic Wine Producers:
http://www.forkandbottle.com/wine/biodynamic_producers.htm

Rainforest Alliance Certified:
http://www.rainforest-alliance.org/about/marks/rainforest-alliance-
certified-seal

Fair Trade Shopping Guide (coffee, tea, chocolate, sweeteners):
http://fairtradeusa.org/shopping-guide

Halloween Candy Buy Back Program:
http://www.halloweencandybuyback.com/about.html

Operation Gratitude Halloween Candy Program:
https://www.operationgratitude.com/halloween-candy-buy-back-2012/

Composting Basics:
http://greenactioncentre.ca/content/composting-basics-and-getting-started/

DECORATION AND GIFTS

Charitable Giving:
http://www.charitynavigator.org
https://www.justgive.org

Fair Trade Certified Gifts:
http://fairtradeusa.org
http://www.serrv.org
http://www.tenthousandvillages.com

Find an Organic Florist:
http://www.localharvest.org

How to Hold a Halloween Costume Swap:
http://www.greenhalloween.org/CostumeSwap/howto.html

DIY Non-toxic Halloween Makeup:
http://www.sierraclub.org/sierra/2013-5-september-october/green-life/nontoxic-halloween-face-paint

Find a Christmas Tree Farm:
http://www.realchristmastrees.org/dnn/AllAboutTrees/TreeLocator.aspx
http://www.pickyourownchristmastree.org

Christmas Light Recycling Program:
http://www.holidayleds.com/christmas-light-recycling-program.aspx

Christmas Tree Recycling:
http://www.realchristmastrees.org/dnn/AllAboutTrees/HowtoRecycle.aspx

OTHER

Environmental Working Group's Skin Deep Cosmetics Database:
http://www.ewg.org/skindeep/

First Day Hikes:
http://www.americanhiking.org/first-day-hikes/

Search Ancestry Records:
https://familysearch.org

Green Dating Sites:
https://www.planetearthsingles.com
http://www.greensingles.com

Purchase Carbon Offsets:
https://www.carbonfund.org
http://www.terrapass.com

Forest Stewardship Council:
https://ic.fsc.org

Non-Toxic Household Cleaner Recipes:
http://eartheasy.com/live_nontoxic_solutions.htm

Essential Oils Guide:
http://www.sustainablebabysteps.com/uses-for-essential-oils.html

Thanksgiving Dinner at Plimoth Plantation:
http://www.plimoth.org/plan-your-visit/shop-dine/themed-dining/
thanksgiving-dining

Buy Nothing Day:
http://www.buynothingday.co.uk

Volunteer Vacations:
https://www.justgive.org/donations/volunteer-vacations.jsp
http://www.globeaware.org/about-us/volunteer-vacations#.
VfHRAs40OFI
http://www.projects-abroad.org/volunteer-vacations/

Index

www.ingramcontent.com/pod-product-compliance
Lightning Source LLC
Chambersburg PA
CBHW072249310526
45795CB00011B/498